12"
99BB

Today's Neurotic Family

TODAY'S NEUROTIC FAMILY

A Journey into Psychoanalysis

by HARRY F. TASHMAN, M.D.

Published for the
Laymen's Institute for Psychoanalytic Enlightenment, Inc.
by the NEW YORK UNIVERSITY PRESS

Library of Congress catalogue card number: 57-8501

Printed in the United States of America

Acknowledgment is made to Mrs. Beatrice L. Cole and to Dr. John Tebbel for their splendid editorial suggestions. I feel a special sense of gratitude to Mrs. Cole for her sensitive and astute reactions to "what belongs and what does not belong."

To my wife, Mildred, and to our son, Michael, and our daughter, Susan, I dedicate this book.

Contents

Book One

Book One

"Man, Know Thyself"

In my work as a psychoanalyst, I frequently see something new come about in my patients—a new idea, a new perspective, a new way of life. But the new is not so easily obtainable as the old and is often difficult to conceive, much less to achieve. Forces operate within us that hold us back. We may lack the power to emerge from their grip. It takes special effort, strength, ingenuity and perseverance to overcome customary ways of being, to grow into something different. But the gains are more than worth the effort.

For my part, I seek the new; and in this volume my hope is to be a guide to the many who seek happiness, well-being and a better life, and to whom I have been unable to reach out in the past.

For a psychoanalyst may be gratified by his achievement in bringing about better realizations for his patients, but he may also be frustrated because time permits him to take no more than three or four new ones a year. Those who are in analysis with me are daring to change, daring to find new horizons to explore, discovering new areas within themselves and new resources to tap. A great many other people have the same pioneering tendencies, but they do not have the opportunity to go on such expeditions as do the patients to whom I am a specialized guide.

When a doctor sets out on his career of bettering and healing, his ideal is not to confine himself to a few people. His desire is to expand his scope of influence, so I am here attempting the new experience of reaching these others whom I can never see in my office.

The kind of realization I intend to set forth is not of an every-day variety. Some of the vocabulary is not to be found in common knowledge nor in familiar language. But one who is seeking new enlightenments should be ready to learn new words and ideas, even though the learning process will not always be easy.

In their highly specialized work, the analyst and his patient form a culture of their own in which communications and understandings come about that are not expressed in common words and phrases, but rather through the language of man's unconscious. There we find written out the hieroglyphics of his antiquity, of all who came before him, and of whatever remains that is represented within himself. All of this must be translated into language that we know.

A few of these words from the unconscious, whose full meaning would be difficult to grasp, will be defined here. The most important word I want to make comprehensible is "symbol."

The American flag is a symbol of our nation. When we see it, particularly at certain times when our emotions ride high, that flag, merely a piece of cloth with a colored design on it, arouses our feelings, our emotions, even our passions, to the point where we would die to defend it. On the other hand, a swastika, again merely a pattern of lines, arouses feelings of shuddering horror at its terrible implications.

A symbol, then, is not the "thing" but a representation of it. It could represent the nation, the condition, the circumstance, the experience, the personality, the happy event, or the catastrophe.

The mind is made up of such symbols, and in the mind of the individual they are as significant as reality itself. In fact, even more so, because the reality of the outside world does not occur to the person at all. It is practically nonexistent, except as it is symbolized within his mind.

We are going to draw a distinction, too, between the symbol and the word, the word being derived from the symbol, but more specifically related to reality.

The unconscious mind is the reservoir in which all that we know and experience exists in unorganized, illogical and irrational form. It is like the raw material out of which commodities used in life are fashioned. For example, to try to use the unconscious where consciousness should be used would be as efficient as to bring a pail of coal into a room, put it on the floor and assume that the room will be heated, or to drag some trees into the house and assume that we will have furniture. Rational thought, which is consciousness, is derived from and manufactured out of the raw material of the unconscious.

There is another concept that needs some explanation. That is the new concept of gravity I am herewith postulating—gravity in the field of time.

We know about the force of gravity in the spatial universe. We know that unless we are supported by something, if we are above the ground, gravity will pull us to the terrestrial base. As infants we are, to a great extent, unable to utilize our anti-gravity capacities— that is, we cannot lift our heads, which fall by reason of gravity's pull. As time goes on, however, we are not only able to hold up our heads in space, but are soon able to hold up our trunks. Later we crawl, then learn to stand erect, be symmetrical and walk. Thus we master equilibrium in the field of space.

We are not accustomed to think of gravity in the time sense, but for each one of us time has a base which begins as soon as we are born, and indeed there is a time base *before* we are born, with which I shall deal later. Our base in time is analogous to the terrestrial base in space. We tend to fall back to that base unless we develop anti-gravity capacity within the moving universe of time.

When such failure occurs, we live in the past. We cannot rise to the present or project ourselves too competently into the future. It is extremely important to conceive of these relative spheres of time, so that we can know how to cope with them for the sake of living, which unquestionably relates to the future more significantly than to the past.

II

Socrates, the greatest thinker and teacher of his time, advised his followers, "Man, know thyself." In the language of today he would be saying, "Get yourself analyzed." Socrates must have been unaware what a great undertaking it would be for his fellow men to heed his advice, or he would not have tossed off the suggestion so lightly.

Today's Neurotic Family

In the first century A.D., Aulus Celsus (53 B.C.-7 A.D.), the first medical historian, whose book, *De Medicina,* was unearthed and translated in 1443, sagely declared that if a physician were really going to effect a cure he should get to know his patient's mind as well as his body. Celsus did not realize that a physician of his time could hardly know his patient's mind without making a study of his own first, and that would have been no less a task than gaining a comprehensive knowledge of the patient's body.

But Celsus must have been aware, so many centuries ago, of what we have come to realize today: that what happens in the body is reflected in the mind, and that the events of the mind are reflected in the body. With this simultaneous interaction and reciprocity of influence, they are really inseparable, functioning as a totality. Celsus was probably the father of psychosomatic medicine, but even today, two thousand years later, many of our doctors are unable to orient themselves psychosomatically.

Meanwhile the amount of knowledge we have accumulated about the body and the mind has become so vast that no man can know all of it. He who tries to know it completely must necessarily forfeit knowing it precisely and, by the same token, he who would know it precisely has to forfeit knowing it completely.

The family physician—the general practitioner who is so important a figure in our community—is, if he is conscientious, already an overburdened individual. The more he tries to learn about what is known, the less he can absorb, to the point where his information must necessarily be spread so thin that it is relatively ineffectual. On the other hand, the specialist has become so much more admired and valued that he is paid twice or three times or even ten times as much as the general practitioner (undeservedly, I would say) for knowing precisely rather than completely.

This, I believe, is the nature of our medical dilemma. It is incumbent on each of us, therefore, to try to gain more knowledge about ourselves on our own—to find out what makes us the human beings we are, why we make trouble for ourselves, and how we make ourselves unhappy.

Since recorded history began, man has striven to know about himself, but as he proceeds in his self-inspection, something deflects him and he is unable to get very far. We have found from our studies of him that in trying to look into himself to gain understanding he not only loses his way but misinterprets. Indeed, he succeeds only in deceiving himself.

For thousands of years, he was deceived by others. In the beginning, man's mind was possessed by sorcerers and witch doctors who told him that the influences accounting for his mental and spiritual nature were derived from remote and irrelevant areas located somewhere in the skies or underground. Heaven was the habitat of benevolent forces; hell was the habitat of malevolent devils. These sorcerers believed they could influence and dominate these forces, good and bad, to the benefit of the patients they professed to be healing and curing. They did so through magical maneuvers—signs, rituals, sounds, cajolery, praise, appeal, entreaty. The devil, which somehow had managed to get inside the poor patient's body to wreak his evil, had to be exorcised, threatened and railed against. Thus the devil would be frightened into leaving the suffering body, while the poor patient hoped and believed in the ritual, sometimes perhaps with skepticism he did not dare express.

For a long time the province of man's mind was in the hands of such groups, who formed hierarchies which became the vested interests of their disciples, descendants and heirs. These primitive theories of man's nature still dominate the thinking of a vast majority of people, even in this enlightened time, and are still looked to with the hope and conviction that humanity's suffering may be relieved by them.

Freud, fortuitously, was not taken in by such nonsense. He set aside the taboos, intimidations and prohibitions and thereby wrested man's psychic life and destiny from the mighty hands of those who had usurped this vital area, and subjected the human mind to a desperately needed scientific investigation. He refused to look to the remote and obviously irrelevant regions in his search for the origins of man's nature and the causes of his mental and psychic ills. Biologist, physician, neurologist that he was, he studied man's mind by examining it directly, observing its phenomena with a scientifically trained perceptive apparatus which afforded him the ability to see, hear, touch, measure and thus realistically compute and evaluate the nature of man's mind, instead of hallucinating about it. Freud ascribed all the individual's ills to the man himself.

Then came those who could not agree with Freud because of their incapacity to investigate specifically and scientifically. Their preconditioning by early unscientific indoctrinations barred them from such psycho-biological investigations. Often their early intimidations and insecurities had generated too much anxiety for them to be able to accept Freud's bio-sexual evidence. These were the culturalists, who ascribed man's ills to society and its institutions and what they demand of him.

We have only to look at the people of our time to see that most of us have been troubled, threatened and in despair. We do not have the ability to master our lives, to be happy or well. Freud gave us knowledge of the personality. He blazed the trail which led us out of ignorance and darkness, but he did not give us the whole answer, nor is the answer to be found in our social structure. As a matter of fact, it was never Freud's intention to give people a panacea; he knew there was much more to be known and explored. Nor do I think that the culturalists believe they have given us the final word about what there is to be known concerning man's mind and its troubles.

In this book we are going to explore another area—that of the family—which is interposed between the person described so thoroughly by Freud and his followers, and society, which has been so abundantly investigated by sociologists and cultural psychoanalysts. We are going to study the family because we want to know more about the nature of the individual, and if we are to discover this knowledge we must examine the sources of the materials that combine to make him. Man is a product of families.

The family is not theology, the heavens or the devil; it is not the individual by himself; it is not society. The family is the point of confluence of all of these. It is that area in which the derivatives or residues of all of these are gathered and represented within the figures which constitute the family. That is to say, the filterings from the past —religious beliefs, mores, cultures, societies and their philosophies, theories and ethical principles—constitute the forces which motivate the figures that make up the family. The family is that immediate area which the evolving human being directly experiences and which therefore constitutes his actual reality.

The family constellation, as I shall term this concept, differs from environment generally by virtue of the fact that it is particularized. Every family is different from every other family, as every set of fingerprints, every personality, or every face is different. The individual has his family represented within himself as he took them into his mind, in the way he takes in food and light and sound. He keeps them there as memories and figures, and mosaics of figures. He is also the precipitate of the natures of his forebears, who were in turn condensations from their antecedents.

This is not such a complex thought when we consider that we all have characteristics derived from our fathers and mothers, and they, too, had characteristics that could have been obtained only from their antecedents. Man, therefore, emerges from his forebears, whose own experiential history has transmitted to him the nature of themselves. In turn, man precipitates a seed out of himself carrying the condensed characteristics which will again flower into an individual from whom the fruit that is the family will evolve in the likeness of the old, with perhaps some modification that is new.

Since the family makes the individual what he is, and since the individual continues to be part of the family that he re-creates, and since history has forged him and can forge him again, knowledge of what his family is made of can be used in the remaking of the individual.

By taking this approach to the problem of self-understanding— that is, through an understanding of the family, the actual reality with which we come in direct physical, spatial, temporal, meaningful contact—we will be better able to look into ourselves to see how we came to be and what makes us what we are, and how we can help to cure ourselves of some of the ills that beset us.

Chapter 2

The Sexual Scene

The purpose of this book is to know ourselves more fully by acquiring a knowledge of our family relationships, past and present. But such knowledge cannot be gained if it is blocked by superstition and obsolete systems of belief, by ideas, jargon or high-sounding words which shut us off from a realistic understanding of what living is, and what it is not. The reader must open his eyes and look at what is evident in connection with life; how life came to be, and the nature of the elements that make it what it is.

To begin at the source, there is the fact that before we were born we lived inside our mother's body. We came to be there because a particular man, our father, during sexual intercourse, ejaculated his reproductive substance into the vaginal vault of a particular woman, our mother.

In this seminal throw, there were contained between two and three hundred million would-be creators of life, only one of which, because of its particular prowess, agility, swiftness and perhaps even good fortune, outdid all the others and was able to reach the waiting ovum, penetrate it and impregnate it, thereby initiating the life process which resulted in our birth.

The preconceptual elements of us, before they became coalesced in the common theme of generating life, existed in bodies entirely separate from each other. These bodies because of a mutual attraction, or by virtue of physical propinquity and the rush of natural urges, were driven to mate. Each offered a specialized part of itself to the other for the sake of reproducing themselves in a new synthesis. This is how we began. This is what we came from.

Man or woman, each a part and possessing a part of the other, is created as the greatest living force on earth. This does not mean that men and women are god-like, but that gods are people-like. One has only to consider the act of conception to understand that here is an actual scene of creation.

In spite of this lofty conception, humanity in general appears to consider that sexual intercourse is an evil and dirty and shameful thing. It is so frowned upon by many that the act actually induces repugnance, nausea, shame, guilt, or feelings of despair and unworthiness. That this is a perverted and depraved reaction to life can be seen by comparing it with that of any of the other families in the animal kingdom. No animal, however undeveloped and low in the scale, suffers from such distortion of the act of regeneration, which is the symbol of the continuity of all life. How this strange and sick aberration, this disarrangement of nature's purposes, came to be man's way of thinking is one of humanity's most inexplicable tragedies. It can be ascribed only to man's inhumanity to man. God would not have thought to put such an aspect on an act which regenerates life.

Creating life is a sexual activity and can be achieved only by a male in combination with a female. In its very inception it is comprised of no more than the elemental sexual products. This is the original gregariousness. The sperm which have not achieved unification and combination with the ovum soon disintegrate. Biologically speaking, it is a self-evident truth that to conceive of, dream of, or contemplate physical or symbolic celibacy or aloneness is to accept death in life, partially or totally.

Because psychic form corresponds to physical form, both being biological manifestations differing only in degrees of complexity, it would be well to examine the physical models in action at the moment of conception. Out of these models psychic forms will evolve, bespeaking our nature.

The ovum, the female, is earthy and round, rich, gravitational, receptive. Life needs to be given it. It falls down to the womb and waits. The sperm does not wait, nor does it gravitate. It has distinctly anti-gravitational capacities. Its flagellum whips it in an upward direction against currents of force. In leaving its former world to find and create a new world, the sperm is active and aggressive rather than passive. It penetrates, creates, gives life.

Out of millions of sperm, the "chosen one" arrives and creates life for itself. The others, even the runners-up, go down to ignominious defeat and soon become inorganic. We can infer that basic and implicit in human nature is the wish to be first and to disregard all others. In adult life, man manifests qualities which are similar to the characteristics of the sperm. He wants to be first and foremost; he wants to win; he wants to be the one and only.

The expression, "A man rounds himself out," implies that he is fully developed. This is the miracle that happens when the sperm enters the ovum. He rounds himself into a living being.

The preconceptual elements ultimately spell out on the symbolic level, the level of the mind, the characteristics of the human being. Of course there is no mentality in the sperm, or the ovum, nor a complete body, but in combination they have the potential to evolve into both body and mind. They become a psychic representation only after much complex development. In short, what man and woman are and wish to be, and what they do, are not unlike what the sperm and ovum actually and morphologically do in all their activities and behavior.

The qualities that characterize masculinity are remarkably similar to those that typify the sperm. Masculinity is anti-gravitational, aggressive, penetrating, competitive, active, migrating, vitalizing, arrogant, directing and creating. By contrast, femininity is round, gravitational, passive, receptive, supportive and creative in an earthy way. Femininity is broad, warm, embracing, stable, non-obtrusive and modest. The male is blatant and warring, boisterous, explosive and meteoric. The female is gentle, soft, subtle, life-giving and constant. The female is an oven, a house and a world. She is also the sea. She is heaven and earth. While directness is a masculine characteristic, indirectness is a feminine quality.

All these morphological configurations possess connotations which achieve symbolic representation in our nature, our mental and spiritual dispositions and tendencies. Each of these qualities or characteristic is, of course, latent in every human being, male or female. Realistically, there is no such thing as a living being that is purely spermatic or purely ovarian, a complete female or a complete male.

The Sexual Scene

The ovum achieved aliveness when it incorporated within itself the form and quality of the sperm. Similarly, the sperm which penetrated the ovum absorbed the form and characteristics of the female. Clinical examination of the fully formed infant shows clearly that the female has rudimentary maleness in its physical structure, and the male, rudimentary femaleness. On the physio-chemical level, it is a fact that male and female each has 20 per cent of secretions of the opposite sex in its blood stream.

As a psychoanalyst, I can declare with certainty that on the level of the unconscious each male also has impulses, fantasies and strivings that are female, and every female has similar opposite characteristics. On this level, too, there is no such thing as pure masculinity or femininity.

The result of this bisexuality has been to create an important difficult problem, the problem of how a person psychically conceives of himself. In spite of his obvious maleness, a man may very well in his unconscious thinking, and because of early experiences and identifications, conceive of himself as a female. Thus he acts roundly, subtly, receptively and passively. In the same way, a female may conceive of herself and act as a male.

Psychosexual evolution and differentiation begin after birth and progress successfully or unsuccessfully. They become either congruous or incongruous with the physical biological structure. When psychosomatic sexual incongruity occurs, untold suffering and sickness may result.

Here we must face the fact that nature has, in a sense, failed us. The psychic potentiality of man has not been given as good an incubator as his physical being. To put the psychic embryology of man into the crude hands of man himself has been to give him an Achilles' heel, a basic weakness which has led him into the most destructive aspects of his life.

Chapter 3
Sperm-Woman—Ovum-Man

To understand more clearly the implications of our preconceptual elements, and how they eventually become latent qualities within us, we must define the nature of "aliveness" and compare it with its opposite, "deadness." It is only when this difference is considered that the characteristic traits of male and female become significant and we can see what their effect will be as expressed in attitudes toward others.

Anything *alive* is an open system, meaning that it is in a state of interchange with environment. To be shut off from environment is to discontinue the state of aliveness. Such discontinuance takes place with all the sperm which did not interchange with the ovum, and it occurs on another level when an animal is shut off from air, water or food. In order to maintain aliveness, a living organism has to take in, retain, give off and reproduce. If any of these prime characteristics of aliveness is absent, livingness is impaired, reduced or extinguished.

Striving is an inherent tendency in all living things, while obviously a dead thing has no interest in what happens to it or within it. It is indifferent; any force can have its way with it. Drop a pencil and gravity takes over and pulls it to a base, but drop a cat and it will resist the best way it can to preserve itself. The primary purpose of the animal is to survive, to defend itself against anything that threatens its living integrity.

In the organic and alive, the differentiating factor appears to be the existence of a set of values, in which aliveness prizes itself over and above deadness—a state shunned, held in contempt, dreaded. Striving has to take place because inherent in living matter seems to be the wish to continue in the alive state, and if that wish is to be fulfilled it is essential that a continuous striving must take place towards environment for materials to be taken in, retained long enough for use, then eliminated.

We strive physically and psychically to carry out all these cardinal necessities that make for aliveness. The wish creates the striving. The striving is for nourishment, not only on the level of the body but, significantly, on the level of the mind.

As in physical metabolism, which is the use of materials and the elimination of waste, we must also rid ourselves of psychic waste on the mental level. On the physical level, man is constantly threatened by his own waste products. In each of his body's hundreds of billions of cells, each one a battery in its own right, the living built-up aliveness and the broken-down deadness exist side by side. The dead materials have to be disposed of, for when they accumulate to a certain degree and displace a proportionate amount of aliveness, they become a threat. Even as riddance of this unwanted, threatening material takes place on the physical level (through bowels, lungs, genito-urinary system and the mechanism of perspiration), so must the broken-down materials that have become symbols be eliminated on the mental level.

But where physical waste matter can be disposed of easily, psychic intake and output can take place only through association with other human beings. For example, a man who feels himself to be immoral because of his wishes and impulses wants to rid himself of these feelings. A most convenient way to rid himself of this concept is to try to induce another human being to feel himself immoral. Then he has the pleasure of feeling moral himself.

Thus it is plain that the individual is threatened not only from within by his own broken-down elements, but also from without by the transmitted symbols of psychic waste from others.

At the time of sexualization, all the other sperm had to be less vital than the "one and only," or he would not have had viability. He might have been the strongest simply because he was stronger than the others, or he might have been comparably strong because the others were weak and, if he were not really the strongest, he might have made himself relatively the strongest by making the others relatively weak. In any case, he had taken away the potential of the other sperm to become human beings. At that time, then, dehumanization was merely a means to survive, a means of himself becoming a human being.

Now it is understandable why the term "catastrophe" is not too strong a word to use for the fate of the hundreds of millions of other would-be creators in that particular tide of seminal fluid, who perished at the very threshold of a life-span while the victor created a life and a world for himself in that tremendous competition. That one triumphant sperm—long, narrow, straight, shaped like a rib, or an arrow, or a meteor—became the creator who would not tolerate another, who would be jealous and destructive of any other and would see to it that none other came before it, with it, or even after it.

Is it any wonder, then, that in the nuclear content of each human being, man or woman, there should be latent and potential feelings of omnipotence?

This dramatic scene, which took place at the beginning of each of us, is a battle between hundreds of millions of living things, each of which wishes to continue to live. The sperm is microscopic, but its potential in the world is incomparably greater than that other particle of matter, the atom, whose power we are only beginning to understand. Moreover, its battle to maintain life begins only after it has achieved that life in a manner unknown to science; thus mysticism precedes scientific knowledge.

In the sexual act, the male element is spectacular in its completely selfish, relentless and all-powerful striving. No sooner does the head of the sperm penetrate the wall of the ovum, however, than the ovum snaps the head off it, incorporating it into its own sphere. In brief, this all-powerful sperm which activates, vitalizes and gives life is immediately absorbed and utilized by another richly endowed life-giver, the creative ovum. Considering the whole act, it is hard to say which has the greater power.

It may be noted here that the scene of conception has its counterparts in the struggles of humanity. For example, the urge to conquer is a basic impulse. That others will perish so the conqueror may enjoy his victory is a commonplace in history. A country is battled for and won. One man seeks to conquer the earth, driven by a madness, an original, primeval, basic motivation that, in my opinion, can be derived only from the original impulse that motivates the sperm to achieve an ovum. An organism, a mother, a land, a nation, a planet: they are all synonymous with dear life itself.

To return to the drama of conception, the sperm spreads itself and its influence throughout the domain of the ovum, and in that sense can be said to dominate it. But the ovum can also be said to have swallowed up the sperm because of the latent hunger that it had for living, thereby dominating it with its own intrinsic qualities.

What happens with the preconceptual elements is not unlike what happens in the mating of a man and woman. One can do to the other, and the other can do to the one; and in the ways in which they affect each other reciprocally we find repeated the drama of the ovum and the sperm. It is obvious, therefore, that there are significant implications to the transaction we call sexual intercourse.

Consider what claims sperm and ovum might make if they could so express themselves. With omnipotence and arrogance, sperm could say: "I have given you life; without me you would have ceased to exist."

With equal truth, the ovum could reply in kind.

The sperm might declare: "I am mighty. I have outdistanced all others; my speed is the greatest. I overcome gravity. I am Atlas."

To which the ovum could retort: "I do not have to chase. I am rich within my own boundaries. I give warmth, protection and nurturing. I give life, and without what I have to give, you would go back to the dust that you were. Though I gravitate, I stabilize and organize. I keep you from shooting your head off and becoming lost in space."

Each from his own point of vantage can proclaim himself to be boss, the master of the other. This is the basic conflict that later, in the marriage relationship, becomes the struggle for power which can be so dividing and destructive in the family. Who will wear the pants? we say. Who grasps the power? Who determines the fate not only of the parents but, more significantly, of the children?

Man and woman could become a unified whole in their mating, of course, but because human beings lack the capacity to go forward and overcome the backward pull of time, they cannot achieve the coalescence and unification to make for harmonious, symmetrical oneness. Instead, there occurs the schism, the defect, the weakness, the point of vulnerability, which later is translated into the disharmonies, disunities and inner divisions which separate people, families, groups and nations. They become houses divided against themselves.

How and why does such disunity come about? Why is it that when connection and combination have taken place, sheer mutuality is not the result? What is the nuclear weakness in human nature that makes for antagonism?

The explanation lies in that *aliveness* which has been won and prized. Because man has to overcome what he was before, namely, timeless inorganicity or deadness, and because gravity exerts its constant pull against him, man has to strive against the forces that draw him back into earth and into the past, in order to maintain his prized, alive state. He must develop anti-gravity capacity in both the spatial and temporal universe.

In brief, man must do two things: he has to avoid the pull of gravity (centripetalism) that would disintegrate him to his inorganic elements, making him revert to the past in the temporal universe; and he must keep himself intact from the pull of an antithetical force (centrifugence) that would draw him out into space, diffusing him and dissolving him into other dead elements. He has to maintain himself as a cohesive whole within his own skin, and to remain a cohesive community of organs and systems. He has to fight against the forces that would make him dead again.

Aliveness is no part of deadness, but deadness persistently appears within the living being, and this he must rid himself of constantly. So long as the struggle succeeds, aliveness can prevail; man continues to remain alive, but when the quantity of deadness displaces a sufficient amount of aliveness, life quickly begins to revert to its inorganic and dead past.

We see, then, that there are antithetical or antagonistic forces in operation within the individual himself, and that everything which takes place in the body is reflected in the mind on the psychic level of the symbol. Consequently, since sperm battles sperm and a body in its psychic sphere can conceive of itself as being of the opposite sex, a woman can, on her psychical level, be spermatic in her aspirations, battling her husband as though both were striving towards the same goal—the ovum, or woman symbol—in order to achieve sexual complementation.

By the same token, because of his early experiences, a man can see himself surviving only as an ovarian being, and insist upon assuming the characteristics of a woman. The way of being is established not only within oneself, but it becomes a force that influences the mate to assume the opposite role.

In the complex business of living together, the goals may be characterized broadly as being or not being, living or not living. Always there are two main themes: one, the theme of you-and-me; the other, pre-existing the first in time, experience, or even in space, the theme of I-alone.

You-and-me means wholeness, harmony, symmetry, peace. I-alone is synonymous with I-without-you; in-spite-of-you; I, the-one-and-only; I, the first; I, the most powerful.

These I-alone attitudes obviously do not result in a you-and-me life. The relationship becomes, instead, you-*or*-I, and the result is division, disharmony, hostility, separateness.

When the partners in a marriage are motivated in their unconscious minds by preconceptual striving towards similar goals, if both conceive of themselves psychically as ovarian, they are striving for the same goal, and, on the level of the symbol and the idea, they are perpetually in conflict, hating each other and vying with each other unconsciously as though the one were about to achieve life and the other were not. In such a situation there can be no psychic coalescence, and no sexualization, because vitalization cannot take place. The couple cannot achieve unity, harmony and happiness.

This is where the schism begins. It begins with the incapacity of the partners to be anti-gravitational in the field of time, so that instead of achieving mutuality after connection and combination take place, they fall back on the forms of the preconceptual state. This weakness can only be explained on the basis of the devitalization of the intrinsic, reproductive functional capacity in the living, pre-conceptual elements. It is the result of our historical suppression, degradation and defamation of sexuality itself—man's dehumanization of his fellow man, just as one sperm in becoming a human being prevents other sperm from doing so.

The weakness in our germ plasm is what one might reasonably expect after the thousands of years during which man has devoted himself to reducing the sexual potency of his fellow man. Such potency is not reduced through physical mutilation of the genitals alone, as in some primitive societies, but in our culture through the symbol or word that is transmitted through suggestion, implication, exhibition of mutilation, command and threat.

For example, a wife may insidiously and through subconscious communication create a conviction within a man's unconscious mind that even though he has the physical form, he is really not a man and the possessor of male genitals, but that she is.

When an individual's symbolic representations or features come into conflict with one another—as for instance when the female conceives of herself as a male—she can only be in conflict mentally, and unconsciously hate her husband. In such cases, a woman has a man around not because she wants him herself, but simply to deprive him of an imaginary ovum or real woman whom he might achieve, and whom she herself, in her fantasy, hopes at some time to acquire for herself.

The animal that is man is a human being only by virtue of his mind, an apparatus with which—on its various levels—he can dream, fantasy, think and know. With this equipment, he has been more successful than any other animal in mastering the world of reality. If this apparatus, that makes him so powerful a competitor to others, can be weakened, or if he can be caused not to develop the great endowment it represents, or if he can be made to forfeit it or lose it, he can be said to be dehumanized and more easily exploitable.

Man is and feels as he conceives himself to be. If he can be devitalized in the psychic areas of his mind by means of the symbol, through implication, suggestion, threat or command, he is weakened in the area which is his greatest strength.

Chapter 4

The Usurpers

A man may have fully developed genitals and yet be completely unable to use them. The reasons for this are to be found in the man's state of mind, the way he sees himself, or feels himself to be. That state determines how he will be able to act, regardless of abilities he obviously should have because of his physical structure. If the idea, or the symbol, declares he cannot use his genitals, that he is not potent, he simply cannot function sexually.

What a person comes to be is the result of his relationship to his family, the way its members relate to each other and to him. He is a by-product of other people's emotional relationships, and, because of his early dependency and helplessness, inevitably he becomes structured by what pre-existed him and by the conditions that surround him. His mind is really not so much an outgrowth of his body as it is an ingrowth—of the influences, themes, ideas, attitudes and ways of life he was exposed to in the constellation that is his family.

Consider, for instance, what may happen to an infant in a you-or-me kind of marriage, which has begun with the common struggles toward adjustment and the hostilities that intimacies between mates engender. Perhaps, as it happens often, they are advised to have a child, in the belief that things will go more easily for them. The arrival of the infant often appears to do the trick, to the general satisfaction of the advisors. But what is not known or seen—worse, what no one seems interested in—is that the hostility that would be directed from one mate to the other is now unconsciously diverted and grounded in the child.

As we have seen, the competition between you-or-me mates results in perpetual hostility because, on the symbolic level, the female envies and competes with the male as the male may very well do with her. An unspoken agreement may now be made between the parents on the unconscious level. In effect, the settlement is that what would have been done to the husband can be done to the child.

If the wife wishes to be dominant and assume leadership and be the doer, the creator, the giver, the usurper of prerogatives and independent activity and aggression, she may now do it to the son and not to the father. It becomes a tacit understanding between husband and wife that she can achieve her symbolic realization of masculinity, by depriving her infant of his symbolic realization of his masculinity. The boy may actually grow up with the conviction in his symbolic structure that he is not a male. In such a situation, a male child may become the sacrificial lamb and come to conceive of himself as being unable to function as a man.

What the child has lost here is the right to handle the motor power of the brain, the motor phenomenon of consciousness which is that part of the mind most able to measure, appraise and judge reality in order to deal with it effectually. Conscious knowledge is of no use unless the individual has built it within himself—unobstructed, unthreatened and unimpeded. It is only when he can take the initiative and use his mind and maneuver it that he is able to forge for himself, to get successfully from the outside world what he needs and give to it what he should.

It is very difficult for a man to have a feeling of freedom and confidence in his strength and vitality if he has been forced into dependencies, subordinations and limitations and has been overruled, or if he has been punished for trespassing into areas that those around him have claimed as their own. As he moves through his daily activities, his range is limited in his relationships to other people, and his freedom of action is made contingent upon surrounding situations and the personalities who have power over him.

Having been belittled or oppressed by his father or mother, teachers, or other authoritarian figures, a man may feel himself small; he may even conceive of himself as having a small penis, although physically it may be larger than normal. In such a situation, he can only achieve the conceptual dimensional superiority so essential for functional psychosomatic congruity by making his wife smaller than himself.

Then he has to degrade her. He looks at her and calls her his baby. He says she is a lovely, sweet, little thing. He gives her the idea that she cannot do anything, that he will take care of her. He laughs uproariously at her inanities and incompetencies, and at the same time he is delighted with his own magnanimity and benevolence. He has grandiose ideas of his own greatness.

For her part, she appears to accept his pretenses, but she really hates him for the humiliation that all human beings experience under the implication that they are small and weak, unable to function like other people.

The case just cited is a gross manifestation of contempt. There are innumerable others. Here is the husband, for example, who professes to be much interested in literature, keeping his eyes on his book and ignoring his wife. She feels unseen, unrecognized, unwanted, alone. He may avoid her in many ways, giving her the feeling of being repugnant or untouchable.

A woman, on the other hand, has her own subtle devices for impugning, belittling, degrading and humiliating by insult or innuendo. The implied sum of her behavior is, "You can't." Sexual frigidity, so common among women today, and so much on the increase, implies to the male, "If you were a man and if you had it to give me, I would react to you. As it is, you see that no matter how you try, and how you pretend to be giving me something to take into me to delight me, I feel no delight. I have no reaction, therefore you have given me nothing. You don't have anything! You can't!"

All this is registered by the woman and the man on the unconscious level, and resentments are engendered which do not manifest themselves directly. Nevertheless they become displaced and result in expressions of irritability, depression, and such psychosomatic manifestations as gall-bladder attacks, migraine headaches, skin conditions (particularly itching), and diarrhea. In the man's case, the result is very often one of the forms of sexual impotency.

To understand the psychoanalytic viewpoint involved here, perhaps it would be well to define both sexuality and love, as the psychiatrist sees them.

As we have seen from our own prehistories, to love implies the attraction of opposites, after which we remove the negativism of the two opposing elements by dissolving, merging, and completely blending them into a oneness, a unity, a whole. An easy comparison is electricity, which can flow and be a force only when there is a difference of potential, when positive joins with negative. Then energy is liberated, power is created and light results. When positive contacts positive, deflection takes place; one repels the other, dispels the other, bombards the other. It is a collision, the force of which can only be destructive.

Love, then, is a compounding, so to speak, a coming together of elements; in its original sense, it is made up of a natural and harmonious composition of opposites. When two such elements combine, adding to one another and making something new, what results is the synthesis we call love. It has to be a synthesis, a building-up, a creation—as we saw creation when sperm and ovum added to each other and created a new life.

The only form of sexuality transacted by men and women that is considered significant in the eyes of society is physical or organic sexuality. Psychic sexuality is not talked about or thought of as such, nor is it engaged in with a sufficient amount of conscious knowledge or freedom. Nevertheless all sexuality means reproductivity, or aliveness, the opposite of which is nonreproductivity, or deadness. One or the other prevails; one either adds to or subtracts from life, and an individual can either vitalize or devitalize another. If an individual's mental quality is such that it adds to vitality and increases survival value for himself and others, then that individual is sexual or loving on the psychic level. But if that quality impugns, degrades or subtracts from another by implication, then he may be said to be asexual, devitalizing or hating another.

We have established that such devitalization occurs because mates do not complement each other, and when this state of affairs prevails there are rivalry, disharmony, antagonism, hostility, conflict and combat instead of harmony and happiness. Instead of the one-for-all and all-for-one relationship, it is a case of every man for himself. Beneath the thin disguise of social amenities, platitudes, courtesies, and pretensions of devotion, the specialized observer sees clearly the battles that go on constantly in the lives of such a couple.

Reproductivity is one of the cardinal features of aliveness. The individual is constantly reproducing within himself, repairing and building. Man constantly re-creates himself, and his creativeness is analogous to his reproductive capacities. He creates physically and symbolically.

The physical and symbolic representations of sexuality are interchangeable. One represents the other, reflects the other, depends on the other. When a couple cohabits physically and there is no psychic, symbolic mutuality, they might just as well be alone. They remain strangers, alien to each other. Physical, sexual activity without symbolic realization is not sufficient for mental and physical health and a wholeness of relationship, even though physical orgasm is achieved. Coitus should be reproductive in its symbolic as well as its physical meaning. Sexuality is synonymous with creativity, although an individual does not have to be reproducing in the sense of having coitus or of giving birth to a child. There are many ways of combining and creating with another.

For example, a body that is abounding with living energy and reproductive impulses reflects itself in the symbol and thereby becomes represented in the mind, which then becomes the motive power that leads the body to another for expression. If the idea expressed is one of aliveness—"I am alive; I want to be alive; I want to reproduce within myself so that I will be alive; I want to have the pleasure of aliveness; I want to be alive with others in all possible ways"—then there is freedom in reproductivity and creativity.

But when the psychic is negative and desexualized in its connotative organization, it will block impulses that flow into it, and relay back to the body that there is no sexuality or reproductivity. In that circumstance, the body will be completely unable to function sexually, and will feel itself cold and sexually dead.

Here the individual's symbolic sphere is expressed in this way: "I am dying. I have been caused to wish to die because I dare not be sexual and capable of love, and therefore I cannot reproduce or per-petuate life. But I do not wish to die. I have to disown this symbolic representation of death. I must rid myself of it. Therefore I wish an-other to be desexualized. If another isn't able to reproduce, then I am able. Or again, if I can't, why should he? If I have been deprived, I must deprive him. The other must die that I may live."

The body throbbing with aliveness relays its urges and impulses for expression to the mental sphere, to be represented there within the shapes and meanings and connotations of the symbol. When sexuality has been identified with dirtiness, sinfulness and sewage in this area, the individual is unnaturally impelled to avoid it. Such unhealthy concepts are the result of teachings or indoctrinations that began in the distant past and, because of the aggressiveness of our forebears, are disastrously transmitted to us and influence the parents who are socializing and giving mental attitudes to their children. Instead of conceiving of reproductivity and creativity as being con-ducive to aliveness, they are symbolized as a threat to aliveness. It is like telling an individual that if he eats he will starve, convincing him of it, and then frightening him out of the ablity to take nourish-ment.

In order to live, even the single cell organism has to divide and re-produce itself, or else it perishes. Since sexuality and its synonym, reproductivity, are cardinal features without which aliveness cannot continue, if there is no connotation of sexuality on the level of the symbol, devitalization and relative deadness occur in the mind.

When such deadness exists, there can be no getting together on the psychic or symbolic level. People with such an affliction become isolated from each other. They cannot be mutual in their thinking or feeling. This is dehumanization: destruction of the capacity in-herent in man's endowment to communicate intimately with his mate, his children, his friends, on the level of the mind. In this state a man and a woman cannot belong to each other because they belong to the systems of beliefs that hold them in slavery by having de-vitalized them.

When such devitalization takes place in the mind, the higher faculties cannot develop. The only modalities that can be used for adaptation are the more primitive, archaic ones acquired millions of years ago and existing in the human brain structure at lower levels. These modalities are capable only of rigidities, stereotyped activity, and automatic repetitions and reflex reactions. These archaisms out of the precivilized past find their way into our present-day thinking as values, attitudes, philosophies and ways of life.

Perhaps the most paralyzing archaism carried into a man's present experience is the nonverbalized command of his mother or father, incorporated in his unconscious mind from infancy: "Be less than I am."

This command may very well (and usually does) restrict and constrict an individual's horizons for life. By using it, the parent achieves relative superiority to overcome the relative inferiority that has been his heritage and constantly threatens him.

Thus the female may command her husband unconsciously, "Be a female so that I may be the male." The wife, as we have explained, may imply, "You haven't got a penis, I have the penis," and on the symbolic level she actually achieves it in hallucinatory fashion by symbolically depriving her husband of it.

In whatever language the archaisms are expressed, there is always the same idea: I am this, therefore you have to be that. The person thus commanded unconsciously registers the command and has to accept it. His response is a compliance: "I will be this so that you can be that. I am bad, and that makes you good, and I have you who are good."

There are many other commands, all following these laws of primitive antithetical part-and-counterpart thinking. They are transmitted not through words or language as we know it, nor as the people who give or receive these commands know about them, but through extra-sensory perception, through innuendo, symbols, signs, vague allusions, suggestions, facial expressions.

For example, a man may ridicule himself, and then notice a happy light in his wife's eyes. She would then be saying to him with those shining eyes that it makes her happy to have him degrade himself. The husband may, at the same time, be saying to his wife: "Be the opposite of me. Be one thing so that I may be the other."

In contrast to the I-am-the-greater figure, there is the worshipper. "Be greater than I am," says the worshipper, "so that I may be able to participate in your greatness, so that your greatness will flow towards me, so that I can receive from you." In brief, the victim arranges to be a failure so that he can receive help.

These elemental archaisms represent the same thinking on a primitive level as that seen in the preconceptual struggle of the sperm to be the "one and only."

When a man has been weakened, and his potency impugned, derogated and therefore degraded, he must dehumanize all others to prove his superiority and assert his omnipotence by declaring: "I am greater than you. I create, therefore you have not created and you cannot, or shall not, create. I am the one creator, the one and only, and there shall be no other."

Without this archaic relativism, such an individual is unable to believe that he, too, is creative. It is the same elemental archaism that causes him to wish another to be devitalized so that he may be vital, to degrade and belittle his wife and children, to deprive, humiliate and degrade others, to tear them down, belittle, impugn and condemn them. This is the origin of such folk expressions, descriptive of relations between husband and wife, as "He makes dirt out of her," or "She makes nothing out of him," or the complaint, "I am nothing; I don't amount to anything."

One person seeks out the other's faults and weaknesses and immoralities—anything to degrade the other. The innuendoes may be too subtle to be discerned by the untrained observer, but they are the barbs that wound and destroy the marriage relationship and undermine the family.

Such degrading attitudes toward a spouse occur only when the person unfortunately has to live a you-or-me kind of life. As has been described, this incapacity is brought about by an inability to mingle and blend on a psychic level with others. Emotionally, these people are the ones who have not been able to mature to the level where they would be capable of sympathy and altruism. Their egocentricity makes it impossible for them to project their libido outside their own boundaries to other living beings whom they would endow with their own warm livingness.

These are the ones who have themselves been so scorned, chilled and degraded in their early days that they could hardly afford any of the life-giving impulses they had to go in any direction but towards the center of themselves. They are "alone" people, pathetically threatened at every moment, precariously balanced in their conceptual spheres between life and death because they have nothing to offer for combination with others. Deep inside of them lurks the panic that is furiously held back by great walls of neurotic defenses.

The kind of panic to which they are susceptible is like the panic of a person drowning. The drowning man reacts to his rescuer with a panic which causes him to fall back to primitive levels of reason, in which the archaic notion is one of the you-or-me concepts—if you drown, I do not drown—and so he attempts to push down the one who is trying to rescue him, and drown him as though that would save himself. It is clear how little survival value there is in this archaic notion of what we might term alternation.

Obviously the drowning man was unable to use foresight and judgment, because if he had, cooperation and collaboration would have been possible and both would have reached shore.

In each man's endowment there is a place in his brain which has the potential to function with special ability to see ahead, to rehearse future possibilities, even to predict what certain attitudes will bring and what events may occur, and so be prepared for them. We all know, however, that judgment has not been man's privilege, nor has he been given the right to prophesy. In the competitions of life, these functions are at a premium, but one does not dare to encroach upon the fields of interest and enterprise of those who would be the prophets or those who claim to be their representatives.

These are not the only functions and powers man could claim and develop if he dared to do so. The ability to perceive and appraise reality, specifically and actually, is latent in the physical endowment of each human being's brain. That brain has billions of pathways for knowing, for receiving impressions, recording sounds, registering light, color and texture, defining, outlining, appraising and experiencing external phenomena.

But on close inspection it can be seen that one human will disallow another, frighten him away, not permitting him to enter and really acquaint himself consciously with the external world of reality. Again the archaism dominates the thinking of the one who deprives the other. If you have it, that means I do not have it. One might wonder how such an elemental and primeval conception could come about. Where does it begin?

To trace it back to the beginning of life outside the womb, could it be that when the infant is at the breast, and the world to him is no more than a breast, he can only think or feel that he has it, or he doesn't have it? If he doesn't have the breast, or if somebody else has it, or has anything that reminds him of a breast, possibly the fact relays itself on the level of the symbol in the adult to the original fear of not having a breast.

Perhaps we should go back farther, and say that it begins with the battle of the sperm, when the language is "Either I get the ovum or he gets it, and he must not have it. I must deprive him of it if I am to survive."

This concept in the undeveloped mind of the infant, which can only reason this-or-that, black-or-white, you-or-I, may prevail and dominate man's thinking mind irrationally for all of his life.

Chapter 5

The Frighteners

The first phase of mental development is a vapor, or so we may conceive of it, and this vaporization is the immaterial occurrence within the infant's brain that materializes again into his dream.

What is this immaterial occurrence? It sounds like a paradox, as though we talked of something existing which does not exist. We are accustomed to speak of materialism and spiritualism, or body and soul. But what is soul, and what is spirit? Where do they exist? What do they come from?

No one speaks of the spirit or soul and implies that what he is talking about is a nonentity. Indeed, the soul of man has been dignified to the point where it is more significant than his body, which is thought to be comparatively unimportant, or at least held in lower esteem.

But the immaterialism of the mind has a relationship to the materialism of the body. Scientific investigation of the rise of man has shown that he has his own life span (ontogeny) during which he evolves, but that he is also the evolved product of the evolution of the species that is man, going back through the ages (phylogeny). All that happened through the ages happens again in the life span of the individual. As Darwin put it, ontogeny repeats phylogeny. Before materialism began on the earth, there existed what we call the pre-materialistic mist, or the evaporation of the waters out of which emerged the dry lands of the earth.

In the same way, the human being keeps re-creating himself from moment to moment, remaking himself into something new: a rebirth is constantly taking place in his mind. The waters of his body, comprising 87 per cent of his total structure, vaporize constantly. This vapor combines with what he is taking in, constantly creating new emergents within himself; his thinking mind constantly creates and grows, and again becomes the new material.

Creation, re-creation, evolution that is immaterial—the synonyms for which are spiritism and soul—occur inside man's skull, out of his own brain, in his own mind.

A characteristic of man is that he dreams. In the beginning, he dreams about himself and the world he lives in. As he evolves, he produces his fantasy out of the mist of his dream. His dreams, through the evolved fantasy, move nearer to the world of reality, and its phenomena are taken into the vapor and mist of his dream, taking form within him in shapes, forms and meanings that at first dimly correspond to those that exist in the outside world.

In this unconscious area of man's mind, his images of the world are not too definitely outlined and differentiated. There are marginal overlappings and indistinctness. Articles, things and people are not too clearly distinguished, nor does man conceive of his own boundaries as being separate from objects. He feels as one with them. If he regresses to primeval ways of thinking in later life, because of sickness, he once again becomes nonspecific, misty, mystical, diffuse and universalized. Again he feels himself identified with all things, all space and all time. He even feels as all-powerful as the cosmos itself and fancies his mastery of it.

When normal progress takes place, fantasy evolves to thought, a realistic limitation is imposed upon the spreading vagueness of his symbols, and a systematic arrangement of the outer world of reality becomes represented within him. Reaching this stage of maturity, he is able realistically to appraise his own dimensions and meanings. When he can do that, then he does not need the compensatory and unreal overexpansiveness that he resorted to through the regressive route. A man capable of such appraisal may be said to have a realistic existence as a human being among other human beings.

Fantasy is derived from the dream, but is more organized and more directed. It is nearer to consciousness, but is not consciousness, and has more than vague outlines of form, objects and motion, and other features of the outside world. The dream and the fantasy are largely comprised of symbols, but symbols are vague, general and nonspecific. One symbol can refer to many things at the same time.

The Frighteners

Let us take an example on the prelogical level: that is, the symbol before it has gone through the phases of development and become the finished product, the word, capable of efficient communication with the outside world in specific terms. The symbol that is an apple could mean fruit, an eye, a breast, something forbidden or sinful, something pleasurable, or even something unpleasurable. All of these can be taken as identities in the unconscious imagery of the individual.

The symbol differs from the word in that the word designates more specifically and accurately what it refers to in the world of reality. Words organize and consolidate consciousness and make an individual more able to deal adequately with the novel situations that confront him.

Symbolic thinking is regressed thinking. It is not suitable for the successful testing of reality. For centuries, however, the human being has been seduced and enticed into symbolic substitutions for reality. He is thus being inveigled into mental sickness.

An experiment performed with a cat indicates clearly the incapacity man may develop when he is reacting to symbols and does not specifically differentiate between the symbol and the word: the word, one may add, which specifically refers to the actual object, the thing.

When food was presented to this cat, a bulb would light up simultaneously. After the cat passed the lighted bulb on the way to the food, a blast of air would strike it and frighten it. After a few such experiences, the terrified cat made no further attempt to reach the food. It had now developed a neurotic phobia, making it incapable of getting for itself what was necessary to maintain its living integrity. When there were no further blasts of air, and the food was in the offing, the starving cat would go no further than to lick the electric bulb, which now symbolized the food, and contented itself with that. Because of its frightening experience, the cat had to console itself with the symbol.

Similarly a mind that has been frightened away and has had to withdraw from reality is compelled to live off the symbol, not the thing. Man's mind, like the cat's, can be conditioned to being satisfied with the unsatisfactory substitute. To help us adapt to the complexities of our life today, symbols are too vague, too inaccurate to be reliable.

It is obvious, then, that if a man's thinking is dominated by symbols he cannot modify his actions and adapt himself through his ability to use specific words. Therefore he cannot act with resiliency or with understanding of the situation, but rather gravitates to the symbolic spread of meaning which can, because of a previous fright, disable him so that he cannot achieve his goals.

The mind that dwells excessively in symbols and imagery is a weakened, sick and primitive mind, driven out of its own higher centers that would have enabled it to function with greater elasticity, appropriateness, resiliency and refinement of action. On that level of adaptive capacity, an individual would have in readiness a repertoire of talents, abilities and dexterities which would enable him to improvise successful attitudes to face every contingency. When he has been deprived of these higher faculties, he is functioning with lower-level systems which are the archaic patterns so inadequate to modern living.

Superstitious and magical systems that promise fulfillment of wishes and needs feed symbols and dwell on them, encourage and nurture them. We experience great delight in the vagaries and mysticism that have such pleasant dreamy qualities. Mythology, fables and fairy tales dwell on the long-dead past and impose upon our present lives the experiences, relationships, triumphs and tragedies of people who were not at all unlike the very people we are and live with. Their experiences are dramatized and popularized to the point where our own experiences seem relatively insignificant.

Yet the principles, laws and values that we are compelled to live by belong no less to the past than these stories. They were appropriate to conditions and situations prevalent perhaps thousands of years ago. They appear today as altogether obsolete, and as absurd to utilize as an oxcart in competition with a jet plane.

But more important is the anachronistic treatment of a human being's mind that forces him to live in time perspectives separated from his actual life by thousands of years. To force the unsuspecting child, when he is ill-prepared even to begin to cope with the extreme complexities of our culture, to orient himself to cultures and events spanning all human experience, not only taxes him unnecessarily, and to no purpose, but as a consequence renders him incapable of comfortable orientation in his own life, and certainly predisposes him to "splitting."

The individual would do well to remember specifically that though symbols appear in consciousness, the words that are derived from them bear direct relationship to surrounding reality, approximate it accurately, and consolidate consciousness and make it efficient. Realizing this, he would then be able to perceive that will and judgment are his natural endowments. If man's judgment and his ability to prophesy are disallowed him, it is because his will nowadays has to be borrowed or obtained from someone, or from some institution, that has appropriated to itself the right to judge and will for him.

Undoubtedly there is God's will, but one may be permitted to doubt that God would will that man should suffer such an indignity as to be deprived of his own will. Again we must repeat that only man would usurp another man's right and hide his predatory design behind a sanctified pretense of having been given his authority for the usurpation by the highest Being: One who Himself cannot be presumed to contemplate such a thing.

Words are what make up consciousness, then, and symbols are the language of the unconscious, which belongs to the past and to the primitive nature of man. The symbol is a device more suitable to adaptation for the lower animals.

A man should know the threats and intimidations that can paralyze him, and that are contained in the symbols with which he cannot cope because he cannot consciously see them. The transmissions through the symbol gain access to his unconscious mind through the lower centers of reception that are beyond his conscious awareness, from which he has been frightened away. Even as the cat cannot eat and starves because it has to content itself with the unrealistic symbolic substitute, so is man unable to function successfully, because on this primitive level he does not have the capabilities that would be his on the higher level of mental activity.

With these he would be able to perceive, foresee, judge, think, and will in his own behalf. Deceiving himself with gratification from the symbolic substitutes, he does not realize that he is depriving himself of an actuality and reality that he could utilize to his healthy benefit, and that he is literally starving in the midst of plenty.

The only reality that exists is the reality that occurs in the mind of man. The reality that a man perceives and conceives of, feels and knows, may not exist at all for his wife, who may not perceive the same reality that is around him. As far as she is concerned, it may not be. If the symbolic content of her mind is that the outside world is a jungle in which one either kills or gets killed, then in spite of the plenty her husband may provide her, she will still live in a state of threat and destitution.

The husband may be both a good provider and a satisfactory lover, giving her everything she needs, including genital gratification, but because of her symbolic orientation she may place an opposite interpretation on his actions, saying that he is "using" her, "ruining" her, or "dirtying" her. She remains cold, indifferent and resentful.

Her preconditioning—the culture that surrounded her in her family constellation, with its taboos and numerous forbidden things—has in such a case constructed a field of symbols which translates the conditions about her into these obsolete values of the past—values that are inimical to healthy living not only for herself but for her husband and children.

Outer reality is rearranged according to the interpretations of the particular set of symbols which exists in the minds of all people. The body itself can be misinterpreted by these symbolic preconditionings. For example, a body that is well-nourished can feel itself to be empty and on the verge of famine because someone's severe glance has threatened, through its symbolic implication, that it will be abandoned and left to starve. The glance connects and is relayed and illuminates again the memory symbol of the abandoning mother of infancy, causing a feeling of fear, of imminent famine and depression, to return.

All of this will be better understood when, in the following chapters, we describe life as it was with all of us in our earliest days.

Chapter 6

The Omnipotent Infant

At birth we are already capable of certain kinds of mastery. But our adaptive equipment is endowed with an infinitely greater potential that could be developed if only we were not impeded from doing so. Observation of an infant clearly establishes that he wishes and wills and does in behalf of himself. He begins immediately to strive, to demand and command that he get the wherewithal by which to live. He evidences the motor activity that should and would develop into consciousness (consciousness is a motor phenomenon). To put it more simply, man has to be active to create his own consciousness—soundness, sanity, mental competency—or else he will not have it.

In those earliest days, the infant soon discovers somehow that he is relatively helpless and dependent but this we must say about him: that even as he instrumentalizes his inborn grasping, howling, protesting, writhing, and sucking abilities, he is developing other talents and modalities to master and thus adapt to his environment. We are inclined to think that the poor little fellow is empty of motive and design, but if we set aside this concept and do without the pleasure of primitive comparativism that causes us to glow in our benevolent and condescending appraisal of him, we can credit him with an ability to instrumentalize in other respects.

We note that he is divisive, and in some kind of knowingness he senses that for every effect there is cause, and he must be able to cause the effects he wishes to come about. He develops appeal and lovableness, for to be loved and wanted is prerequisite to the effectiveness of his other talents. With the infant, love is the primary security device he possesses. To be loved means that he will be fed, cleansed, kept warm and free from harsh and injurious influences and irritants, be tenderly touched, moved and rocked. Lovableness, sweetness, charm, pleasantness, cuteness constitute his stock in trade, and they are the achievements by which the infant makes himself secure, and by which he attains prestige and a feeling of self-confidence. In later life, these constitute the sole attributes of infantile people who live by mastering the arts of dependency and receptivity.

When these qualities cause changes in the reality about him, the infant is a happy being. But when they are ignored, he laments, cries and develops physical disturbances, all of which express depression or pessimism about his abilities to survive.

If he is successful in making his mother or the mothering one look at him, touch him and attend him, then he becomes reassured. If, unfortunately, she lacks the ability to relate with natural love to him and is therefore isolated and cannot reach out to her infant, or if she ignores him, disapproving and rejecting him, he experiences a fear of annihilation. His fate is entirely in her hands. He proceeds, however, to develop the ability to control, even to dominate, the mother, appealing to her through her susceptibility to his winsome ways. If she does not love him, he develops devices to influence her through her own guilt feelings and anxieties. He screams threats at her. He produces skin conditions which communicate to her that her contact with him irritates him. He vomits to show her that she turns his stomach, and he develops diarrhea to tell her that he would like to get rid of her as she would like to be rid of him.

As time goes on, his mother in the outside world becomes part of his inner world—his dream life, his fantasies, his theories and thinking. Now he relates to her not only in the world of reality, when she is physically present, but in his inner world of dreams, memories and fantasies, where he also seeks to achieve mastery over her.

Thus we see the infant living in two worlds: the outer world when his mother is there, and the world of memories, dreams and fantasies which he resorts to when she is not there. He has in effect two regions, the actual and the imaginary, from which to draw the stimuli to sustain himself with what he needs. These stimuli are specifically those of light, sound, taste, smell, touch and the imaginary that are recorded within him as remembered stimuli that can be recalled again.

If his mother is not there and he needs her, he can call on the memory stimulus to his visual apparatus, or the gustatory or the auditory stimuli, to satisfy and so appease himself.

The infant, then, is an hallucinating, make-believing, fantasy-forming creature who is able to live not only from the realities but from the symbols of the realities that are within him. If he cannot draw from the outside world what he needs, he can resort to the inner world of dreams to feed himself. This alternate, substitute way of life is normal and natural and appropriate for the infant. It is an escape from the pain of frustration caused by not having what he wants or needs from the world of reality. The escape was provided by nature to assuage the tension and panic concurring within him when his mother did not arrive. But nature meant this defensive apparatus to have only limited usefulness.

Sometimes these recourses are resorted to later in life because the individual cannot bear the frustration and limitations imposed by reality or society. He then gravitates to infantile forms of appeasement and comes to depend on this easy way out. Such a person can be said to be psychically ill.

Make-believe, dreaming and hallucinating normally end when the infant's hunger pains become too sharp or his discomfort is too severe. Then he wakes and demands and commands that the real thing be given him. If he is so ill-fated as to be born to an unloving mother, his demands and commands are ignored. He continues to make them to the point of exhaustion, after which he experiences a collapse that is the equivalent of impending or actual disaster—death—a fear that remains deeply imbedded in his roots. Having once known that feeling, he may forever after include in his anticipations the possibility or probability of catastrophic happenings.

The kind of mother who would bring about such a situation is the one who, in later days, encourages him to believe in the power of the wish, the practice of fantasy substitution for reality gratification. She will let him know that it is all right and perhaps even wonderful to make-believe and hallucinate; these are the magical defenses against the panicky feeling of imminent disaster.

Make-believe and the more consciously directed fantasies are normally experienced between the ages of three and six, taking the form of games with fire engines, pistols, or dolls, and playing house or doctor. But the fantasy life of the child at this stage should normally give way to reality testing. When excessive indulgence in make-believe activities are engaged in beyond this period, it may lead later to a predisposition to serious mental derangement and even psychotic processes.

When the mother leads the child to believe that wishing strongly enough will bring the things he wants, that "wishing will make it so," particularly in the face of realistic deprivations, he is encouraged to resort to make-believe and will not be able to distinguish clearly enough between fact and fancy.

In the normal infant, when fantasy can no longer appease him, he wakes from his wish-fulfilling dreams. He feels himself threatened, injured, disintegrating, and at this moment, he experiences the feeling of hate. He feels his mother to be the cause of his suffering and his pain and the threat to his life. He wishes to rid himself of this feeling of doom, conceiving of his mother as having it within her to produce for him that which will relieve him. He wants her to give him what he needs as strongly as he wishes to relieve himself of what he feels. He theorizes that his mother, by relieving herself of what she has, will relieve him of his pain and his feeling of disintegration. How can he force her to do this?

When his mother finally appears with food, the infant believes that what he needs to relieve himself of is what she wants and that he caused her to come to his aid by the hate he felt. He does so by reason of his cause-and-effect theory, and because of his wish to be motor, masterful and effectual, achieving a synthesis of all these elements because of his natural tendency to instrumentalize and his ability to theorize and hallucinate.

What she gives him makes him feel good, but he does not differentiate between what she gives him and what he gives to her. What he gives her is aggrandized in his imagination, though in reality it is the hate, pain and disintegration that are his riddances and deadness. What she gives him are love, food and life.

Grown-up people hate, too, for not much more reason than

that they have been unable, or not allowed, to develop maturity and still remain infantile, so they feel the way to get what they need to live by is to hate, and so force another to bring them or give them what they need. Such people have nothing to give to others; they only wish to take. They are the grandiose ones who overevaluate the nothing that they give and imply that it is important, although in reality they are giving only riddances.

A man may hate his wife, and it is obvious that the reason he hates her is that she frustrates him. The hatred can be ascribed only to the hope that someday he will be able to influence her to give him the things he wants, as he got them in infancy. Because he is still dominated by the feeling of helplessness and dependency he had at that time, he demands that she do for him.

If he could only say to himself, "She doesn't give me the cup of tea I am wishing for because she is preoccupied, or for some reason she is unable to do it. Well, I'll get it myself, as I can get other things for myself." If he proceeds to do so, he is being motor, conscious and able; he is "grown up" and therefore does not have to utilize the archaic device of hatred to cause things to be brought to him magically.

In extreme and unusual instances of regression, an individual may be driven by this hatred to commit what is known as a sex murder. The motive is his need to dispose of his disintegration, disorganization and deadness by giving them to another, believing in his deteriorated mind that these are what the other person wants. Having committed the act, he achieves the fantasy gratification of his own survival. This is one of the byproducts of the reduction of men's minds to a primitive and infantile level. It may account, too, for the senseless slaughter and annihilation of masses of people in nations ruled by dictators.

II

During infancy, the baby is taken care of merely because he is lovable. For the infant, this is living by divine right. Just being lovable and wonderful makes life good for him. But as he becomes older the healthy mother asks him to give more than that. She tells him he must control himself. He must, for instance, control his urine so that he won't inconvenience her too much. At this point she is asking him to give up his divine-right claim to easy and unhampered release, to function according to the reality principle and begin to do his part. He doesn't like it, although he wouldn't mind doing it if she really loved him.

To win the favors of an unloving mother, however, he may pretend that he enjoys doing this for her, but deep inside he does not, any more than we enjoy giving up special privileges which we haven't had enough of, and for which we will get nothing in return.

As the infant develops, his mother becomes internalized and organized out of his remembered visualizations of her and then exists within him as a figure corresponding to the real mother. He now sees her in his mind's eye as two figures: the good mother and the bad mother. The mother who is good comes to him and gives him what he needs and causes him to feel good. The bad mother deprives, threatens, punishes, rejects and may abandon him, causing him to feel bad.

He may react to these internalized mothers in two ways. To the mother-image who loves him (his ego-ideal) he says, "Yes, I will do this for you willingly and happily because we love each other." He aspires to this ego-ideal.

On the other hand, he says to the threatening one whom he fears and hates (the super-ego), "Why should I do this for you? I am not going to surrender any of my divine rights. You do it for me. I will force you, as you force me, without sufficiently loving me."

When he is already pessimistic because she is alien, cold and hostile, he cowers and shrinks from her. Yet to see himself in his mind's eye in any way she would disapprove of—that is, to see himself as having characteristics or traits she would condemn— would be as though she were turning her back on him, and so he has to pretend he is willing to cooperate.

These two mother figures, the ego-ideal and the super-ego, become permanent institutions in his inner mind, and he reacts to them for the rest of his life. People whom he relates to in later life become identified as ego-ideal people whom he aspires to and loves, or they are the rejecting, oppressive, frightening ones whom he avoids and hates, but to whom he may have to be obedient. In socializing him, the loving mother must, of necessity, put a contingency on love. She says, "If you don't control yourself and do your part, I will take some of this love away from you." With such a mother, the child is ready and willing to collaborate because he cherishes what she gives him.

When the unloving and rejecting mother demands that he do his part and he rebels, her threat may spell doom. He is forced to cooperate and becomes automatically obedient; her word or wish is his command. But when these negative demands are doled out with disinterest and indifference, or are not given at all, his obedience is equally impersonal. It has no meaning for him. His responses are stereotyped habits which he has to believe are what he likes and wishes to do. His love for her, and later for his fellow human beings, becomes a pretense, shallow and empty.

In such a case, it does not take the child long to realize that his parents are most interested in their own guilty feelings and anxiety, and he can dominate them because of this interest. In order to punish and frighten them, and thus intimidate them into giving him what he wants, he will feign illness. He will scream and hurt himself, throw himself on the floor, hold his breath and turn blue, injure himself to force the attention and care he demands, and thereby dominate the activities of others.

This utilitarian behavior is practiced by primitive tribes in frenzied religiosity to influence, threaten, frighten and control their gods, who are the projected equivalents of their parents. It is practiced in our own civilized society in more restrained and modified forms; that is, self-restriction, self-denial, self-punishment and self-deprivation in order to appease and win the favor of gods who are the projections of the original malevolent parents. It is also practiced by infantile adults who will go to any extreme to control or procure the attention of others, even if it means endangering their own health. They will use, unconsciously, the psychosomatic

43

mechanism of arthritis to limit their powers of locomotion. In extreme cases, they will even come to the point of committing suicide.

Some mothers are predatory. They conceive of themselves as weak sperm figures who can achieve power only by symbolically depriving another of it, thus becoming the first and foremost. If no one is around to stop such a woman, she will not give her evolving child the opportunity to strive toward an anti-gravity upwardness and thereby develop capacities appropriate to his age which could only result from his own initiative. She will put no contingency on love, on the self-deceiving basis that she does not want to strain the child, wishes to spare him pain and not injure his feelings or make him suffer. She gives him neither positive nor negative sanctions for his accomplishments. She showers him with attention and does for him, but does not let him do for himself, implying that he cannot.

Thus she has discouraged any development of his motor apparatus, and, as we have seen, it is the motor power of the flagellum of the sperm that enabled him to be the first and the one to achieve the ovum, thereby continuing to live.

The predatory mother consequently causes the child to grow up without knowing the difference between right and wrong, without a sense of responsibility or pride in accomplishment. He becomes a social fatality. His mother has nothing to fear from him now in the field of social relationships or in her spermatic fantasy of "the great competition." She will always have to be his protector, his superior, and will therefore be first in her own fantasy, while he remains subsocial and dependent on her because of his inferiority and helplessness. He will always be the underling and becomes the asthmatic, the ulcer patient, and the man who suffers from psoriasis and other skin conditions, as well as the one who is predisposed to many other psychosomatic and psychic disorders.

In the neurotic family, if the mother is not the predator, it is the father who is the inferior one, striving to overcome his inferiority by reducing his wife or his children, whom he sees as competitors. The cards are stacked against the child in this kind of family relationship. It is impossible for him to grow up without a threatening, oppressive super-ego of his own, to which he must constantly make hypocritical pretensions that he is good, noble and pious. Since he knows himself in his unconscious mind to be lying to this threatening, punitive, omniscient, omnipotent parent (conscience), and because he so badly fears abandonment and destruction, he must continue to deceive himself about what he basically is, even in later life.

The newborn infant is pulsating with superlative aliveness. Since it is contained within its own boundaries and has no ways to distribute this aliveness outside itself, it is a creature of self-love (narcissism). Everything within it is over-evaluated, enlivened, even its own inorganic elements, the used-up and broken-down deadnesses within itself, its own excretions.

We have seen that life is made up of sexual elements at conception, and the body evolves out of them as it develops. Consequently it is reasonable to think that life itself, considering the nature of its origin, is permeated by the quality of the life-giving elements from which it is derived.

At birth the pleasure of living is condensed at the localized zones where the outside world is touched most significantly, and for the first few years the pleasures of living (erotic) are mostly confined to the alimentary canal. At about three years of age, we know that the pulsating aliveness and lovingness of the infant become localized in the genitals, and then the infant strives toward objects with actual sex urges and wishes. It can be said that the objects—that is, father or mother, male or female, are a matter of indifference as compared with the urges that seek to be discharged. The infant has only one aim, and that is to enliven and endow everything he touches with the overflowing life and love that manifest themselves as sexual activity.

While behaving naturally, the infant at this time is startled and alarmed to discover that his sexual activity frightens the mother and that it is punishable and dangerous. Therefore, by necessity, he must soon find recourse to secretiveness in activity and to palliative fantasy.

At this juncture there may be powerful withdrawals from the objects in his constellation—the parents or siblings. Now expression cannot be free; no longer can he do naturally and sincerely as he wishes. He has to pretend, to hide in whatever devious ways he can devise so as not to offend others and therefore be offended himself, in order to carry on the natural sexual function that surges within him and pounds and drives at him for expression. He is now made to feel seriously guilty and is severely threatened and injured in the area that will later be his sexual and reproductive organization.

If he is too badly shocked, threatened and frightened at this time by parents who themselves have been too severely shocked and frightened, the child falls back and may forever remain at the pregenital level, or what we might call the level of gastrointestinal libidinal organization. Because he cannot express any of the inflowing tides of urges and impulses, he is threatened by feelings of tension and pressure that mount within him to the point where he feels he will literally burst. Children scream rapturously when they hear a balloon burst because they feel a relieving reassurance that something else burst and not they.

To avoid this painful feeling and fear, the child develops the same kind of phobia that prevented the cat from taking the food it needed so much for survival. The child, then, has to recoil to the previous level of libidinal orientation in which life's pleasures were free to take without threat or punishment, and he repudiates higher integration not only in his body but simultaneously in the symbols represented in his mind.

If his parents could contain their own fears and terrors and observe the infantile sexual phenomena with sympathetic understanding and with knowledge that no real harm could come of it, they would love their child and altruistically reassure him. They ought to understand that it is merely a passing phase and deal with it by using reasonable and kindly techniques, mildly suggesting the improprieties while teaching, with modified and graded attitudes, that, although such impulses and wishes cannot be realized, there is nothing wrong in being what the child has to be.

46

The Omnipotent Infant

The child who is fortunate enough to have such parents retains that original warm flow which undulates and pulsates within him, and later becomes the human being who loves others, expressing himself through love of beauty, the creation of music, art, or the poetry that throbs itself out of us.

But instead the child too often is shamed, shunned, terrorized and punished so that instead of inheriting, from his childhood, sexuality that is whole and integrated, he inherits a body of sexual impulses—a body that has had its head knocked off. Thereafter he gropes blindly through life and social relationships. He is like a ship with a damaged rudder, sailing lopsidedly on turbulent seas with no hope of reaching other ships for help. His mental, symbolic, sexual lights are extinguished and he forever lives in the darkness of disallowance. He has been forced to forfeit that part of his living mind that would have enabled him to reach out, to relate, to live and love, to blend and be mutual creatively on his psychic level with others and his near ones and dear ones.

It is on the level of the symbol that the child had to withdraw— from one of the cardinal features of aliveness, namely love, re-productivity, sexuality—and be isolated and alone because of this forfeiture. It is on this level that he suffers in his association with others. The remaining psychical development continues to progress but in this cardinal respect his symbolic area has stopped growing. He goes into life with a mature body, but with a symbolic organization that has been cut off. He is sexually and emotionally crippled— in a word, infantile.

Chapter 7

The "Split" in Man

Few men remember their childhood in any detail, yet if one observes children it is plain that they are having very real emotional, physical and mental experiences. In later life, however, this period is largely forgotten and cannot be recalled. Why? Because all that is fiendish, savage, ghastly and villainous occurs in the mind of the infant and child, and if it continued he would find no place for himself in organized society. He would be ostracized, hounded, arrested and isolated.

We have to make ourselves into what society expects of us: right, ethical, good, loving, law-abiding, honorable people, regardful of others. But underneath, in our deepest layers, we were the ones who wanted to take the good out of the other and give back the bad. To have enough self-esteem so that we will be optimistic about what society or those about us will be willing to give us, we must see ourselves as the better beings we try to make ourselves out to be.

A man has to deny to himself that there exist in his roots the precivilized savagery of his beginnings and the occurrences that took place when his sexual impulses led him into experiences that caused him to feel so horrified and horrible. This is why man has to deceive himself about what he was, basically. Finding out the truth about that part of himself which he has forgotten, hidden or denied, would terrify and disorganize him from within.

There are three phases in the sexual evolution of the human being. The first, the age of infant sexuality, is from infancy to six; the second, which we term the latency period, occurs between the ages of six and thirteen; and the third is the age of sexual maturity.

The "Split" in Man

During the latency phase, the child is asexual. Sexuality as such is put to sleep, as Snow White symbolically was put to sleep for seven years. During this period, the sexual energies of the child become diverted to, and utilized for, the processes of education and socialization.

At puberty the glands have matured, and as Snow White is awakened by the prince with a kiss, sexuality begins to throb again and there is a resurgence of sexual fantasies, impulses and drives. By that time, the adolescent has developed systems of social values. During the preceding period, the mores and value systems of the culture have become his ideals, his principles and ethics, and they govern the thinking in his community of associative ideas. When sexuality returns, the uncivilized and presocial tendencies and wishes are completely unacceptable.

As we have said, man's childhood is split off and hidden from himself (repressed) because he cannot bear to think of himself as the savage he was before latency set in. He represses the period of infant sexuality, drawing a curtain of forgetfulness over this period in his life.

But the child that he was remembers and feels itself to be a being within him. A life did take place in man's childhood, a life that was colorful, significant, dramatic and supercharged with emotions and passions far more poignant than the experiences of adults. As a living entity, it had survival interests and still strives to perpetuate itself, leaping the gap, thrusting itself into the world of the man it wishes to be part of, asserting itself and often dominating him who is trying to shun and banish his childhood from his consciousness.

The child in man has to live the humiliated life of the renegade who molests, strikes, retaliates and runs away. Vindictively it sabotages whenever and wherever it can. It may be as detrimental to the grown-up the man is trying to be as an anti-social force would be in a community. That hidden renegade is the subsocial or corrupt element within us. It is the unsocialized, socially unassimilated, untutored, violated infant and child who still clamors

49

within us for the discharge of impulses, the realization and gratification of its wishes.

Ethical and philosophical schools of thought teach that man should love his neighbor, care for his brother, help the poor and weak, understand and respect the other person's rights and needs, and love others. These would be the natural tendencies and attributes of the evolving human being if he were given the opportunity to develop.

The tendency of living matter is to spread itself with life, to make another living being able to survive. The sperm wins life by giving it, as does the ovum. The giving of life, which is analogous to sympathy and altruism, is quite as natural as it is simultaneous with getting it. Consequently, if living processes were allowed to mature and develop spontaneously, every human being would develop sympathy and altruism at a certain age, about six or seven or eight. But interference may take place, and when a person in power comes along and insists on disposing of his mental concepts, forcing his words and ideas into another's mind, thereby usurping the area where the individual's own buddings and flowerings would naturally evolve, the victim does not have the opportunity to materialize himself in the logical sequences of his maturing processes. As a result he becomes not a natural, sympathetic, altruistic personality, able to create and love, to give and take, but an automaton, artificially contrived, a person whose psyche has been rudely and crudely moved in on so that his own instincts and his own life streams are obstructed.

II

The central nervous system, the most significant part of which is the mind (the apparatus for adaptation to environment), necessarily has to be characterized primarily by cohesiveness, organization and integration in order to be efficient as a system. When there is a division within the system, there is a breakdown in efficiency. The disunity that takes place in the mind of man because of this blacking-out of his childhood leads to the weakening of the adaptive apparatus, causing nervous and physical disorders.

The "Split" in Man

By virtue of the mind that is his inheritance, and has taken millions of years to build, there is in a man a wonderful potential for creation and love. It could be realized if he were let alone to develop his natural resources without the interference of the crude handling of parents, teachers and other usurping figures. But this letting alone would have to begin from the moment when, as an infant, he began to reach out to do in behalf of himself, to master the world. Instead, the indoctrinators not only tell that child that if he does something in the outside world that is sinful (sexual) he will be punished or found guilty, they go further and assert that even if he has the idea, which is now referring to his own inner world, it will become known. Thus he is frightened away from his own thoughts as well. The phobia (fear) which causes him to cower and shrink from the symbols and ideas occurring in his own mind is projected into the outside world, where he also has to avoid them.

Because of this inner fear, the signs or symbols connoting sexual activity must later be strictly avoided and the individual's scope is necessarily limited and constricted, for if his perceptive apparatus hears, sees, smells, touches or comes to know anything that would remind him of his infant sexuality, and its associated terror, a trigger mechanism is immediately set off that releases the anxiety, recalling to him the feelings of painful pressure and bursting exactly as they happened originally.

As a consequence, he becomes a person who has to avoid new ideas, new knowledge, anything that had previously been unknown to him because of the dangerous implications which might occur. Such a man must demarcate his activities severely; the lines of his enterprises must be rigidly maintained. His behavior must be stereotyped so there may never be an irregularity, and he is compelled to be orderly, clean, assiduous and conscientious. His body and mind become bound, and he must do the same thing over and over. Living has to be according to ritual, ceremony and convention, and all others around him must be the same.

Even his children must not stray from these orthodox confinements, because if they do, and he sees them, hears them, or knows in some way they are doing so, his identification with them re-awakens within him the same symbols and signs that will threaten him with annihilation. Neither he nor his children can project themselves into the future. The precepts, concepts, ritual and cere-monies of the past are cherished fanatically, and must be strictly adhered to.

This man becomes like a horse with blinders. When the blinders are removed, the horse sees a field much broader than he is ac-customed to or can bear. The additional stimulation of his visual apparatus floods him with anxiety and throws him into panic. The human victim must continue to wear his blinders and insist that all others do likewise.

We have now described the orthodox, asexually-oriented indi-vidual who cannot change, who does not dare to take on a new field of knowledge or absorb new ideas, and will not allow anyone else to do so. This refusal is not out of malice, but derives from the fact that he finds it completely unbearable to endure anything more than his obsessive, compulsive, magical defenses against terrible suffering.

Such a man can be recognized through his manneristic peculiar-ities. He is living, in reality, at the infantile level when he relied for his securities on the magical motions, maneuvers and gestures he endowed with such omnipotence; when he believed, because of his earliest cause-and-effect theories, that if he moved his hand or made certain lip movements he was controlling his environment, the people in it and the universe about him.

He dispelled fear by hating; and being confident the hate brought his mother to him, he still believes he is mastering life and achieving survival through these modalities of infancy.

When he lives according to the superstitions of people thousands of years ago, man is ill-equipped, on the face of it, to manage his life. As we live our lives, we learn through trial and error what is good for us and what is not. Our mental arrangements are derived from the happenings within ourselves. The natural energies that emanate from our beings charge our respective levels of adaptation to the highest integration of specific words and concepts that correspond accurately to conditions, objects and situations in the outside world.

The human being reacts simultaneously on all the levels: the body, which produces the dream out of which the fantasy emerges; and the symbols, from which emanate the words, phrases and concepts he creates. When all these synthesize, the individual can live a successful life to his gratification.

But when the word is not the end product of all that he is, has experienced and comes to know, and when it is not the final product of the wishes intrinsic in his own substance, but is an imposition from the outside (indoctrination), then such an individual has not been allowed to live his own life nor to have his own experiences or natural evolutions, nor to make his own security and happiness. He must live according to the instilled, hammered-in words that were the products of other people's lives, words that spare them of their pains, tensions and archaic incapacities.

These words that he is forced to live by are empty of meaning to him. They are not part of his own body; they do not actually communicate with his own biology. They are like foreign bodies, alien invaders, that usurp his God-given resources.

It is clear how important it is for man to develop the higher centers in his brain, through which he can perceive reality correctly in ever-broadening perspective and with appropriate readiness. Only thus is he able to develop his own mind and live his own life in the present.

He could prepare for the future if he could build his own words, but when the old words are forced into him, with their implicit restrictions and phobic limitations, then there is no forward tendency in him. He becomes the reactionary and the bigot.

He is taught that it is wonderful to believe and to have faith, yet he does not stop to ask, have faith in what—believe what? He cannot ask this question, and he dare not, for fear that he might get the answer, and the answer would wake him up to the reality and thus force him to give up his morbid, mystical gratification of infantile dependency. The main reason we lend ourselves to the orthodox ones and their obsolete ways of surviving is due, usually, to this infantile dependency on the initiative, foresight, judgment and will of these magical helpers. If we grow up and become mature, we can create our own world and not have to ape those who came before us.

We should begin to suspect that the prestige one acquires by worshipping his ancestors, accepting the tenets of the past, is a matter of having been intimidated and driven out of one's knowing mind and into dependency for the easy comfort of having someone else do the thinking; of figuratively being carried around on someone else's shoulders. The pride one shows in ancestor worship is a cover-up for shame. The submissiveness always conceals resentments and hatreds.

It is necessary for the desexualized, devitalized man to believe that the father or mother, or the reasonable facsimiles of these, meaning an institution or a system of beliefs, will continue to deliver to him what he needs. These figures convince him that he needs them in order to make that delivery come about. Thus, by lending him crutches for life, the usurpers gain access to his mind, his beliefs and his confidence, and so are able to exploit him.

The way this is achieved is to reduce or disallow the growth or maturity of the individual through the symbolic representative that is essential to the thriving function of the brain cells, namely, the function of reproductivity.

In the gastrointestinal orientation of the child, as we have said, the conception is that the world and its objects are eaten, disintegrated, used-up and broken down to inferior material associated with deadness. This material, he is taught, becomes disgusting, repulsive, to be loathed and forgotten.

Later in life, the pregenital personality relates to people on the psychic level in ways that correspond to the gastrointestinal level, in what may be described as gastrointestinal attitudes. That is, people are good or bad; nice and sweet, or they stink. The individual himself, of course, is the desirable one who is good and sweet. All the others have no sweetness to give or are disgusting.

Such people keep looking for these traits in others because they are constantly finding them within themselves, as products of their own threatening disintegration, and because they cannot be optimistic about their own symbolic re-creation, reproduction, creativity, and self-perpetuation. They feel threatened by death constantly, and so they are compelled to see rottenness, contempt, everything that is bad, in others.

They degrade and disintegrate others as food is disintegrated and degraded when it passes through the digestive system and is eliminated.

Chapter 8

The Desexualized

The man and wife who love each other and exchange positive feelings, interests and influences, also use each other's symbolic systems to dispose of unwanted, painful concepts about themselves. When these psychic riddances are excessive, and the balances of their relationship shift to a degree where hostilities overbalance affections, one or both may rebel. At such a time, a tacit, unconscious agreement is made that the humiliations, degradations or destructions will be discharged onto one or several of the children. In them they have the perfect scapegoats, the ideal whipping boys—defenseless, unable to strike back.

This is a dismal picture of mates and their purposes and intentions toward their offspring. But as one who has sounded out his own depths and roots through having been psychoanalyzed, I find it easy to say that, basically, deadness occurred in me the very moment after my birth, and existed side by side with the livingness in each of the billions of cells that comprised me. The fate of these deadnesses had to be that they would be disowned, gotten rid of, to insure my own survival.

As a human being, I have avenues of disposal no different from those of anybody else, and psychically, if I live and breathe, I take into my mind the symbols of me; I retain, give out, love or hate. I do not credit myself with a purity and virtuosity that would elevate me above anyone else. My children—before I knew better, or beyond my conscious awareness—undoubtedly had to suffer from the transmissions through me from my own forebears.

Only when I stopped to examine myself, intently and with perspicuity, could I determine how much they were treated by me with condescension, grandiosity, excessive protection and humiliating implications. I can only pride myself on doing them less damage now than when I was ignorant of the facts. Getting to know more and more, day by day, I find myself giving better grades of things to others than the day before.

The examination that comprises this book, then, is of the family as it refers to all of us, myself included. It encompasses all our families.

Actually, if we examine ourselves, we are antagonistic to the society of children. We impugn them, ridicule them, take away their rights. As the old saying goes, children should be seen and not heard —a common, if unconscious, expression of our antagonism, which is the projection of that antagonism we ourselves felt in the childhood we lived, and still live in the repressed unconscious. Repressed, it constantly threatens to return and distress us.

If you say to a man, "Don't be a child," he not only feels insulted, but it is true that you meant to insult him. As stated before, we have to forget that we were children, though in our basic life we were children, and for the most part are being children now, though at the same time we deny that our promptings are those rooted in our earliest childhood experiences.

The family is the socially enforced and organized integer that, combined with other families, constitutes our society. It is the socially accepted vehicle through which man's reproductive function and dream of self-perpetuity can be carried out legitimately. The legitimacy of it is constituted by his ability to be responsible for his sexuality, which includes the products of his sexuality: his children and their socialization.

Schematically, or topographically, not much more can be said about the family than the above. But as far as the study of the nature of the minds of the people in it is concerned, and how these respective minds came to be what they are, how they influence each other, and what can be done about it, we find ourselves involved with a primary concern which is much more complex.

The family is a group of related individuals. Relatedness again is on the physical, physio-chemical and mental levels. It begins with mating, which in our society can be engaged in with impunity and security, for the purpose of having children. It carries the promise of survival because it is only through progeny that man really enjoys the healthy and happy fantasy of after-life and immortality. True immortality and true after-lives come about through the symbolic representatives of ourselves, the product of our seed.

Identification with his children relieves man of his dread of deadness. He identifies himself with his children and through them projects himself into living at future time. As for after-life, it is the solace of the celibate and the desexualized. The sexually able individual reproduces himself, and sees himself in his descendants who paradoxically project him into the future. Even though he has children in the physical sense, if he is psychically, symbolically asexual he cannot identify with them, so he remains the unfortunate, isolated celibate who has to be given the solace of a life in the hereafter. So do his wife and children.

In reality, a family is that unit of society which consists of related people: the head of the family, who presumably is the father; the mother, and the children; and also, probably, aunts and uncles. But whatever the family consists of, there is always one dominant figure.

In medicine, we study anatomy and physiology, which represent the normal. Then we study pathology, which is the abnormal. A normal family would be one in which psychology and biology would have been congruously inherited by the respective spouses, who make the new family and congruously transmit that wholeness of being which is in harmony with nature. But, as we said at the outset, when man was given his mental evolution and his sexual differentiation and identification to work out for himself, he got into trouble.

The desexualized man, meaning a man incapacitated in his higher mental integrations, cannot maintain his grasp of the present, with all its implications. He regresses and falls to his predifferentiated form; that is, to his pre-established, undifferentiated sexual identity.

Between the ages of three and five, he could have aspired to his heterosexual objects. The boy could love his mother and identify with his father, and when he grew up, he could be like his father and do as his father did and get a wife like his mother, whom he would love. The girl could do the same thing with her father.

But when the growing child is frightened and must avoid totally the period of experience and differentiation because of dehumanizing parents, he has to fall back and remain undifferentiated. In that case, as far as the psychic level is concerned, the boy does not have it settled in his mind, "Am I a he or a she?" Neither, of course, has the girl.

The marriage becomes the arena in which the struggle takes place to determine who is going to be what; who is going to be head of the family and live the role of the father, and who will play the role of the mother.

This struggle for sexual identification, which carries privileges, values, credits and their economic advantages and disadvantages that serve as threats or promises of survival, is continuous. Though the respective mates have common interests, they also have individual interests and tendencies to fall out and be competitive, because they are diverted in their individualistic aspirations. A you-or-me life ensues.

How do the children fit into such a scheme of things? They may become the pawns of the contention between the goals of the parents' original aspirations, or they may be the targets of the envies and hostilities that cannot be expressed conveniently to the mate. The children become the vessel in which the conflicts that exist around them are ingrained, established and perpetuated.

A girl, who quite naturally identifies herself with her mother, can be identifying with a power-driven woman and thus become capable only of the role of the dominate male. A son who identifies with a passive, receptive father develops accordingly. When primitivisms obtain in which archaic antagonisms rage between the parents, the daughter is enlisted by the mother into the ranks of the society of the females against the males, and the son and father vice versa.

If a family is oriented to the level of alimentary function, life is thought to be a matter of what one eats or does not eat; what one should eat and should not eat. People are classified and valued, admired or condemned on the basis of whether they are good eaters or bad eaters. The eating function dominates the interests and enlightenments and the goal-directed activities of everyone in the family.

At the other pole of this orientation is the family which esteems or prides itself on cleanliness, orderliness, regularity, materialism and endless accumulation of wealth. These family constellations are often primarily concerned with bowel action. "Did you move your bowels today? When did you, how many times, what kind of bowel movement did you have? Do you need an enema? . . . Take a physic. . . . I don't want to move my bowels." These are among the common expressions.

The family capable of higher-level mental relationships is characterized by intelligent altruism and sympathy, by warm and vital and conscious communications that blend and harmonize, integrate and intimately associate. It is a healthy, thriving family in which sharing takes place for the gratification of one and all.

Contrarily, when the family is incapable of higher-level mental function because of psychic and symbolic desexualization, living takes place on lower levels which are characterized primarily by the separateness and aloneness of all its members. In such families, hierarchical gradations are prominent. The proverbial pecking order obtains. Allocation of good and bad is in accordance with what position one has in the hierarchy. Distributions of prestige, privilege, advantage, disadvantage, pleasure that is gratification, frustration, anxiety, shame, guilt, pain—these are all relegated by the principal patriarch or matriarch, whichever dominates the constellation.

These families invariably draw their influences and patternings for precepts and concepts from their forebears. Orthodoxy is the rule; precedence is rigidly adhered to and automatically authenticated. The tenets, precepts and concepts handed down from the past are a shrine before which zealous worship is conducted. These relics are never questioned or challenged but are completely depended upon. Security is achieved by total submissiveness to them.

The past lives on in such families as though it were life-giving and itself alive, while the future is avoided as though it were death-dealing and degrading.

The Desexualized

It has been said that man cherishes the past. This is not true. It is simply that those who lived in the past and cherished themselves were not able to identify with the creative lives of those who came after them, and diverted their descendants to themselves by investing them with their words, concepts and limitations. So, forcefully and predatorily, they perpetuated themselves into the future, where they are decidedly unwanted.

As noted before, an inorganic and dead thing is something that anyone can have his way with. It has no interest of its own, nor any capacity or evident wish to struggle against the pull of time. Consequently these sons and daughters do not and cannot know that one does not march ahead in life by marching backward, and that down is not the same as up.

One of my very sick patients, who was extremely orthodox in his orientation and was given to such contrariness, said to me during an analytic session: "And so I was walking towards the bridge and thinking of my uncle, who was such a great educator, and I wanted to be like him. I thought that when I got on the bridge, I would throw myself off."

Independent ability to get into motion is one of the connotations of life, but this man did not distinguish between the survival value in going up, and the lack of survival in throwing himself down.

An inference might be drawn about the meaning of this fantasy activity toward achievement. In fact, a theory may be postulated about how a man, identifying himself with a higher-up to whom he aspires, would achieve his wish by "throwing himself down," in the way we have described the fate of the ovum—dropping, falling by gravity, waiting to meet the anti-gravity sperm.

It can be speculated that in the archaism of this man (which dominated his way of thinking in so many other instances) he did not conceive of himself as the man he was—a sperm-producing being—but, since his uncle was the important one, he had to shift to the basic opposite.

One may conclude, therefore, that when men are primitive in their thinking or relating, their attitude towards the one in power becomes that of the female to the male.

The Neurotic Families

The neurotic family is like the preconceptual scene as we have described it. A dominant figure, self-seeking, basically disregarding all others, is on the horizon, striving toward the goal of being the first, foremost and only, seeking for a promised land inevitably unattainable. It is as though the life he is living were not life at all, but a life that someday, somehow, will come to be, perhaps in the hereafter.

In such a man, the pull of gravity in his temporal universe has caused him to fall back to his preconceptual isolation. Because of a lack of vitality, he has not been able to maintain his grasp on the higher level of coalescence, but has had to fall to a previous level of time and character.

Actuality and the present are bypassed in such a person. Although conceived in mutuality, he was unable to live it in the ovum, in the body into which he developed, or with the woman he eventually married. In the preconceptual element that he was, however, there must have been the intrinsic wish that exists in all living matter to remain in the alive state. The hope and wish for life persist, but supersede life itself and project themselves into the future as only a hope and a wish.

Because of regression in the field of time, the dominant figure still conceives of himself as alone and remains so, self-seeking, disregarding all others, living in the past or with vague hopes of glory in a hereafter. The actual living present is a nonoccurrence as far as he is concerned. Further, and by implication, those who are the subordinates in this hierarchy which he heads can only have less than he of the actualities and realities of living experience. It may be called a life of shadows—this dream of living a span of life rather than life itself. It is a perpetual struggle towards hypothetical goals.

In the matriarchal neurotic constellation, the wife strives constantly to invade and appropriate features and qualities that should be the husband's. Whenever possible, she has to be on top and in control. She has to have the last word. Everything he does, she wants to do better—play golf, make money, have a career, have a vote, be a soldier. She wants to pick out the suit he should buy. She buys him a tie; she wants him to sit quietly while she makes love to him. If he initiates activity, she says no, waits a few minutes, and then says "Now." If they have an appointment, she comes late, subtly and without words implying, "You can only stand still and wait while I move towards you."

She wants to have materialistic possessions. She wants diamonds, mink, and money in the bank. She wants, too, that he should have a hard time of it and should not get as far, which allows her the antithetical fantasy of getting further, more quickly. She degrades him in the morning by not giving him his breakfast, saying in effect, "You are not worth getting up for, or I would get up for you." He makes his own breakfast, thereby carrying out her wish for his humiliation and emasculation. Thus he marches out to do battle in the world of business and affairs, having been cut down to size, so to speak. These implications, connotations and innuendoes reduce him in his conception of his own virility, potency, and confidence in his own strength and effectuality.

In such a marital relationship, there is obviously no common ground of mutuality, sympathy and living for the sake of the other as well as for themselves. The relationship is too grim in its competitiveness and individual exclusiveness to be transacted through conscious intelligence. The interchanges have to be beyond the level of awareness. The transmissions from one to the other consist of submental materials, namely, anxieties, guilt feelings, shame and primitive aggression such as sadistic and masochistic indulgences.

One person becomes the martyr who lives out a life of self-sacrifice from which is derived the gratifications of grandiosity and self-righteousness. The other may then be living the gratifications of the elated infant who had, by divine right, been well-fed.

The giver of good things proves in his own secret ways his superiority over the receiver, striving to achieve gratification for himself vicariously through identification, but all the time hating the one to whom he is materialistically giving. At the same time, he is depressed because he really does not receive the gratification he is trying to get through giving. Such a provider may be compulsively, rigidly benevolent with his family, but may select one of his children upon whom he will take his full measure of revenge. That child will, in subtle ways, be taken over and made into the incarnate vehicle through whom the father can live out and experience his selfish aims.

The son or the daughter, then, acting out the father's repressed impulses, will be made into an anti-social being, disregarding the rights of others without the inhibiting force of guilt or shame. He becomes the check forger, the psychopathic liar, the black sheep of the family.

The father appears bewildered by all this, protesting his innocence, harping on how much he has given, not only to the boy but to the rest of his family, to the church and community. He cannot understand why his son turned out so badly.

In the deep unconscious, there is an instinctual relationship between this father and son that is rarely reached, even in psychoanalytic practice. In it these two are engaged in nefarious intimacies so hate- and guilt-ridden that they are terrifying to each. They must necessarily be bound to one another, like two criminals standing together against the world.

The mother who has been humiliated and degraded by a husband who conceives of himself as insignificant may live out her revenge through the living experience of a taken-over and indoctrinated daughter. Such a daughter, hating her father, identifies herself with him and relates herself to other men with the superficial seductiveness of the female, but with underlying hatreds, destructiveness and competition, as when one sperm vies with another. One must lose and go.

Then there is the family with the three classical stratifications. It begins with the grandmother, who woos her church for comfort and love. Her daughter hungers for the love the grandmother does not have and is trying to get for herself from the church. The mother, continuing to woo her own mother, necessarily deprives her family of a mothering figure. She will develop masculine powers—a powerful mind, material possessions, and other masculine equivalents—to win her mother's love. The grandmother, however, has developed the same kind of prowess to win the love and security of her church.

There are no real mothers in this type of family. The church is used as a source of power which the love-hungry grandmother wields with tyranny and oppression rather than with mothering warmth, nurturing and tenderness.

At the end of this line of descendants is the young daughter, who did practically no maturing at all, and who doesn't evolve much beyond the level of preverbal expression. She becomes the young person who speaks the language of the body. She is the asthmatic who clings desperately to the air she has taken into her lungs and refuses to exhale it again. The air represents the mother who may never return once she leaves. Again, she may become the patient with ulcerated colitis who constantly attempts to rid herself of all rivals for her mother's affections whom she has symbolically devoured to get them out of the way.

Consider, too, the family in which the father has to prove his masculine potency to overcome a feminine identification with his mother and busies himself chasing after women half or one-third his age. Such a family has no authority figure with whom to identify. The members are left to scramble for themselves, becoming involved with every stray figure who happens to appear within their scope—evangelists, rabble-rousers, and other spectacular pseudo-idols. Their enthusiasms are as quick to fall as they are to rise, and they never form a stable, organized personality of their own.

In another neurotic constellation, the father has to take flight in some kind of activity that will consume his energies, because of his inability to have a mutual relationship with his wife. By reason of their competition, they have become dangerous to each other. He may go into politics to save the nation, leaving his own sons to become unstable, derelict, even criminal. His wife, driven by her own power-seeking aspirations, heads the local Parent-Teacher Association, while their daughter becomes more and more infantile, regresses, and even becomes deranged for want of a mother.

Then there is the father who has inherited or amassed a great sum of money which eclipses and dwarfs him and makes him its lackey. This man uses his money to reinforce and extend the range of his muscles. He wields a mighty fist and uses it to browbeat, beat down and knock out anyone who stands in his way. Values like justice, ethics, philosophies, beauty, or love are as unknown to him as they are to gold itself. He buys everything and anybody, and sells anything or anybody, and comes to have the spirit and soul of an ant.

Another type of neurotic constellation is the super-educated family, in which the intellect lives rather than the person. Intellectuality is used as power, as money is used as power. In such a family, intellectual achievements are acquired not to enable the individual to live more broadly, warmly, and sympathetically with others, but rather to prove that others are inferior, to be looked down on contemptuously.

This kind of intellectuality is a substitute for incapacities and inabilities to live mutually with others. In fact, it is very often a manifestation of the desexualized individual. Because of his pregenital orientation, the member of this family must constantly prepare himself with more and more college degrees, learning and preparing, but never knowing, doing, or living a life of responsibility.

The father of such a family may have been a child prodigy. He was, perhaps, the little boy who was smartest in the class, exquisitely alerted so that he wouldn't miss anything, but never realizing that what he was afraid of was that he would miss his mother, which would give him a feeling of having been abandoned. To overcome the insecurity and apprehension of that eventuality, which he had once experienced, he must know everything there is to be known. Nothing must be unknown, because that would spell out the knowledge that he does not know where his mother is.

He becomes the man who looks down on materialism from below. He does not realize that the theorizing and thought-juggling he does, theorems he proves, and the philosophies he builds, are merely compensations to overcome the frustration of not having been able to achieve success in the material sense. He constantly calls the grapes sour.

This father, of course, cannot provide his wife and children with the actual necessities, and his spirituality is essentially and obviously distorted. His wife and children see through him, resent him, and pity him. In our field of understanding, however, pity is merely a refined term for hating. He and his family would certainly have been much better off if he had dealt realistically with his situations and not become the mental gymnast. He would have been better off, and so would his family, if he had become a simple plumber or carpenter.

There is also the neurotic family in which the father or mother is threatened with serious mental derangement. The threatened one has to utilize one of his offspring, in whom he sees the sickness occurring, thereby convincing himself, on the basis of the archaic alternate, that he is not the one who is or will become deranged, nor does he have to fear that he will be the one.

In my treatment of such a "sacrificial lamb," I have found that when the patient begins to advance toward reality and mental health, the member of the family who was the original mental case, and for whom my patient was the archaic alternate, then begins to show his mental derangement. I might add that this is very often a serious hindrance to the process of curing the victim.

The resistances and complexities that arise when I try to achieve final cure with such patients, coming from both the patient and the ailing parent, are so immense, extensive and complex as to threaten seriously and sometimes even put an end to the analysis and further effort. This is, in fact, the subject that led me into the special field of studying the family constellation.

The cured patient in such a case could say to the afflicted one, "The derangement I had was really yours. You were well because

I was sick. Now that I am getting well, you are becoming the sick one you were originally."

Soon after treatment begins, it becomes obvious to me at whose behest the patient is being the mentally sick one. Early in the work, I make preparation in anticipation of the resistance to curing the "lamb" that will arise from the mortified parent who sees more and more clearly that the externalized alternate is going to refuse to be the sick one so that he can be well.

Grave and serious distortions prevail in the type of family constellation where the wife wanted to be a man, and so found herself a weakling husband whom she would make into a man. She constantly throws up to him his weak beginnings, tells him how she made him, how she wants him to be *the* man, and gives him every opportunity to be so. She berates him articulately and irrefutably because he misses this and that opportunity. She tells him his judgment is poor, points out how he fails to make the grade, and explains how she can help him. He lends himself to her manipulations and assistances. He becomes the henpecked one, but he has most insidious and effective ways of his own to get his revenge.

He grows vague and seems not to understand, appearing stupid and forgetting some of the groceries he was supposed to buy, exasperating his wife beyond endurance. He knocks over a cup of coffee that happens to spill into her lap. Accidentally he steps on her foot or his elbow pokes her in the ribs. During sexual intercourse, he lies on top of her like so much dead weight.

The children of such families, especially if they are boys, are like people living in a dictatorship. They wear all the external expressions of good will and pleasantness; they are well-regimented but empty of sympathy towards one another. They are like trapped rats in a ship that may sink at any moment. They envy each other, and underneath the veneer of cordiality, hatreds and death-wishes against other members of the family prevail.

We turn now to the family in which the husband is a well-organized, intelligent businessman who is conscientious in his work and has been brought up with no reason to be excessively suspicious or captious about anything or anybody. He meets a pretty girl who he thinks is cute and adorable. She is a wonderful dancer and is crazy about her daddy and mummy; they are simply crazy about her. She is nineteen or twenty; he has a beautiful convertible, and they elope. Ten or eleven months later, they have a baby. Twenty years later, their baby becomes my patient.

The daughter is a frightfully sick, unorganized, unstable and unrealistic young person whose adjustment to reality is so flimsy and tenuous that on the slightest provocation or smallest frustration, reality is lost altogether.

Investigation discloses that the father, who is still intelligent, still working hard and successfully in his business, with many business associates and friends who respect him, has been completely dominated by his infantile wife whose emotional age level is about one to one-and-a-half years. Her relationship with her daughter has been one of bitter rivalry. Any mothering she gave would constitute her own deprivation. Not only did she deprive her infant of any tenderness or love, but through her temper tantrums, hysterical fits, anxieties, headaches and other complaints, she dominates her husband. Worse than that, she has created a situation in which father and daughter do not dare to get to each other without first obtaining her permission.

This infantile mother has such complete control over her kindly and wholesome husband, and has him so hoodwinked, that he fails to see that she not only is murdering the mind of his daughter right under his eyes, but she has completely inactivated him so that he has no strength to do anything about it.

Let us consider now the family in which the husband wishes his children to have the wonderful mother he did not have but always longed for. He realizes the fulfillment of his wish by conceiving of his wife as that wonderful mother, which she is not. Being unable to bear disillusionment, he puts her on a pedestal beyond question or reproach. Hers is the sanctified role of the inviolate madonna.

In this home, all that is corrupt, underhand, tyrannical and indecent happens to the children at the hands of this over-privileged, deified woman who comes to feel herself to be the wonderful one who can do no wrong and who is always right.

The father, who is still the athlete at the age of forty or fifty or sixty, dashing out to play tennis or keeping fit by feats of endurance, usually calls his wife by such nicknames as Slugger, Pal, Queen, Butch, or perhaps a boy's name. In one instance I recall, a husband who ordinarily called his wife Bobby would call her Robert under stress or when anxiety overcame him.

In this family, the athletic prowess which constitutes the "masculine protest" invariably conceals underlying femininity that seeks masculinity in the mate. The children of such families are usually confused about their sexual identity, and frequently refer to their mothers as "him" and to their fathers as "her." Homosexuality of a more overt type frequently appears in the children of such parents.

But let it not be thought that we have described all the types of neurotic constellations. That would take volumes, because each constellation differs from every other. We have merely introduced a few to indicate how a certain theme may characterize a family, much as basic themes occur and recur in a symphony or an opera. When we can be as oriented to life as the musician is to music, we will be able to visualize or recognize the nature of the theme that has grooved itself into us, and grooves us into the lives we lead.

ᔕᔕᔕ Book Two

Child of a Child

The neurotic family produces neurotic children, who in turn produce neurotic families. Thus when an individual comes into analysis, he always brings with him the inner world that is unknown to him—the constellation he has internalized in his early days and which lives on in him as memories.

These memories are latent and strive constantly to be externalized, to be lived again as realities. The patient may still be living with his original family, or else with the new family he has created for himself, but the new family can be, for the most part, only a reproduction of the old, living itself out in him over and over again.

It becomes obvious to many a patient that instead of his living his own life, as he may reasonably think, it is being lived for him by the natures of the people he has taken into himself in his earliest childhood, and with whom he still identifies himself. One can no more treat a patient as a person apart from all others than a surgeon could remove an organ from the body and treat it as though it could be made healthy independently.

The realism of psychiatry compels me to see my patient not only as a unique individual, but also as part of a unique family. His improved functioning in the psychoanalytical process has to take place both in the area of the self, and in the larger area that is the family.

Not every patient's family grows in understanding as does the patient. In fact, they may have no capacity for change, nor any interest in being different. When that is the case, the factors that relate to the family and its relationship to the patient (factors which very likely have to do with his sick state) become clearly known and understood eventually by the patient. It is then up to him to make a decision. Does he want to make himself a martyr to the general cause of the family? Or does he want to strive for and accomplish independent freedom from the influences that are making him sick?

When Sarah came under my care, I knew that some day she would have to make that kind of important decision about her original constellation.

Sarah was twenty-six years old when I first saw her, and she was at the end of her rope, mentally and physically. Her medical doctor, a gastroenterologist, had called me into consultation as a last hope; he had informed her family that she would die within twenty-four hours. As one who had practiced medicine for many years, I was ready to agree with this prognosis. She had suffered ulcerative colitis for eleven months, and death seemed inevitable.

The gastroenterologist was eminently qualified to treat her. He had used all his skill and knowledge, all the antibiotics and medicines and techniques known to his specialty in the effort to save her life. If my orientation had been in the same special field, I could have done no more. But my education and experience had taken me into another aspect of medical knowledge and practice, so I was able to rally the little life this moribund patient had left within her, and help her begin the long climb back to physical and mental health. Though her recovery was spectacular, there was nothing magical or miraculous in what I did, and any psychiatrist with the proper knowledge and training could have done the same for her.

I found Sarah slumped down in her bed, propped up on pillows. In one of her nostrils was an oxygen tube, and in her mouth another tube carried vitamins, minerals and other nutrients down to the stomach. She was being fed intravenously at the same time.

What was there for me to say to this already collapsed patient? Any words I spoke would have been like hammer blows. When we hear it, a word can only be known to us because we have the strength within to build its meaning. This girl had no strength with which to build.

74

I did not ask her how she felt. I knew that in her unconscious thinking, and out of her unconscious wisdom, she would have said to me, if she had had the strength: "You stupid man; can't you depend on yourself to know? Must you ask me, when I'm so sick, to provide you with the information?"

So I did not ask Sarah how she felt, nor did I produce any words for her to work with. I merely sat in front of her, allowing her to experience the company of another human being, on the most primeval level, and to participate in my tranquillity and optimism. These influences would have been undone by any kind of word. I saw that she was uncomfortable in her position. With deliberate and studied carelessness, I got up and lifted her head, rearranging her pillows and putting her in a more comfortable position. There was nothing in these movements that might communicate the idea that I was thinking, "You poor, pitiable thing. I must be tender and gentle with you, otherwise you will fall apart."

What was implied in my action plainly reached her, for as I sat down, still saying nothing, she smiled at me feebly and I smiled back.

"Am I going to die?" she murmured.

"No," I answered her, without a moment's hesitation.

There was a long silence. Then she said: "Everybody else expects me to die."

"Why should you concern yourself with the expectations of others?" I asked mildly, and I added quietly, without excessive or protesting emphasis, "I don't expect you to die."

These words were not as unimportant as they might appear to anyone who had not made a special study of the subtle forces and dynamic influences contained in certain words at certain psychological moments. These particular words, the way they were timed and stated, tilted the scales and caused this moribund patient to change her direction and take the first step away from death.

This dying woman understood instinctively what is known by newborn and very young infants. She knew that the one who was in the room with her, who communicated with her through an understanding and sympathy (empathy), in the wordless linkage through which infant and mother communicate, had the wish and the will and the ability to help her live. That was all she needed to shift from her pessimism and surrender toward optimism and a fight for life.

Not much more than that took place in our first hour together. Next day she greeted me with a smile that was a little more vital, and it was easy to see she had more tone and color. Little by little, more verbal communication came about, but only at the rate and rhythm and quality of which she was capable. She was the pacemaker; I supported.

In a month she was able to leave the hospital. After resting at home for a week, she began to visit me for regular analytic sessions. After three years and a half of analysis, she was discharged as cured.

Before further details of the analysis are gone into, however, perhaps it should be emphasized that from the moment I met this patient I gave her love, a kind of love that can be defined only by stating what it was not. It was not hatred, hostility, destructiveness, degradation or humiliation. Such connotations were absent from my pantomime, my attitudes and my words.

This positive way of relating to a patient is a highly specialized ability, one that only the well-analyzed, scientifically oriented, intuitive and sensitive psychoanalyst can have. The essence of it is to know how to keep one's psychic symbolic riddances out of one's communication with a patient. Sarah had gotten so much of these riddances from others that she could scarcely have tolerated any more. I would not have been capable of doing it if it had not been for my own laborious efforts in the study of myself, and the subjective enlightenments given to us by Sigmund Freud.

The story of Sarah, however, properly begins not in her sickroom but outside its door, where I encountered her father when I made my first call. Apparently he had known of my arrival, because he intercepted me outside the door. He rushed up to me in a state of high emotional excitement and, wringing his hands, implored me to save his daughter's life. Falling to his knees and weeping, he declared, "I'll give you anything—anything—only save my daughter."

The psychoanalyst is specially trained not to be carried away by the emotional tides of others, knowing that hysterical activity is contagious. He must be aloof from such influences so that he can maintain his objectivity and appraise the situation. I concluded that Sarah's father was simply intent on stealing the spotlight; he was being the attention-getter, the attention-grabber, superfluously dramatizing himself.

Studying this father objectively, I had only to ask myself whether, as a doctor, I would be more inclined to deliver a greater quantity of what I had to give his daughter because he had displayed his primitive and infantile emotional state. Wasn't he aggrandizing himself, I asked, to presume that these histrionics could affect me so that I would be willing or able to do more to help his daughter? Obviously he was doing nothing more than relieving himself, discharging his affects (emotions) to nobody's benefit but his own.

I was not surprised, therefore, when much was said in later analytic sessions about this father who never missed an opportunity to be the center of attention in his home, in just such dramatic bursts that were not always plaintive and beseeching, but more frequently of the type that commanded, threatened and violated.

As the analysis developed, it became clear that the constellation Sarah had lived in was one of emotional scarcity. Her mother, who had been dead a year, was the matriarch of the family, and like all matriarchs she was the child of a matriarch. Sarah's mother had to seek mothering for herself, running frequently to the grandmother, who was lord and master of all her descendants' domain. This old woman ruled arbitrarily with a despotic hand. She appeared to consider it her divine right to dominate, tyrannize, oppress, deprive, usurp and subjugate.

Sarah was one of the casualties in this hierarchy of power. Her mother reported regularly to the grandmother for approval, reassurance, direction and instruction. No opinion, guidance or care could be given Sarah unless it was first authenticated and permitted by her mother's mother. Confidences that Sarah attempted to share with her mother were inevitably transmitted to the grandmother. Whatever maternal supply Sarah got from her mother was contingent on what kind of supply her mother could get from the grandmother.

Nor was this the worst of her deprivations. In order to gain respect and admiration from the grandmother, Sarah's mother had to compete with many others, acquiring powers that the power-driven matriarch would admire. She had to develop a strong mind, strong enough to teach others how to develop a strong mind, and so she had become a schoolteacher. But as a teacher she was with other children in Sarah's earliest days, instead of being with her own child. She did not live out the role of a mother with her little girl, but rather she was a child showing off to her own mother to earn recognition and approval for herself.

If Sarah's mother had no natural mothering to give her children, no more could be expected from the father—this attention-getter and competitor—as we have seen him. He was a bookkeeper, neither very good at his job nor successful in it. His wife would never have selected him if he had been too much of a competitor for her own spermatic fancy.

In this situation, Sarah had to compete with her father for whatever emotional crumbs might be about. There was also an older brother who had to suffer, famished for the love and warmth of a mother who was either at school teaching other children or wooing her own mother to get praise.

Sarah's longing for her mother consumed her. All other relationships were shallow and meaningless. She saw her father as a dangerous competitor who would use his natural prerogatives aggressively and destructively towards her, without once according her the benefits of fatherhood. She saw her brother in somewhat the same light, at least as a competitor. Consequently she came to feel that a man was someone hateful, and certainly no one to get anything from.

In analysis, she recalled the furious battles between herself and her brother. Once he accidentally smashed her nose while he was swinging a bat. As she told me this incident, Sarah's hand automatically reached up to her forehead and her finger ran down a scar made, she said, when her brother threw a glass at her.

The breaking period in Sarah's life began when her mother became an invalid about four years before her death. It was then she understood the stark emptiness and unmitigated parasitism of her father and brother. Now she had to save her mother—to love her, enliven her, care for her. Not even the grandmother could be counted on to supply any warmth or succor.

During this period, Sarah won her infantile battle—the struggle for reunion with her mother. Having won it, she unconsciously determined that this oneness must never be undone, and in her unconscious mind, as I came to know it in analysis, she concluded that the way to live henceforth was to return to her mother. Immediately after her mother's death, Sarah experienced a month of elation and overactivity, her frantic effort to ward off the depression that threatened. But depression did come, and three months of it yielded to the ulcerative colitis which would have led to fulfillment of her unconscious wish to join her mother.

II

On the couch, Sarah was particularly guarded and unproductive. I had told her that if she wanted ultimately to achieve full mental health, she would have to think, remember, fantasy and dream her way back to her earliest days. That, I told her, could best be accomplished if she looked away from me in another direction so that her attention would not be distracted by anything I said or did or the expressions on my face.

The psychiatrist's function is a unique one. He succeeds when nature fails, and realistically we all know that nature occasionally fails. The doctor helps his patient to go back and actually relive his mental evolution, to evolve in a better world than he had with his parents, who were ill-equipped to nurture and influence their child's growth and development. One might say that the psychiatrist becomes that better incubator so that the ungrown or regressed individual may ascend again and evolve emotionally and mentally to levels he would naturally have reached if he had been provided with sufficiently healthy give-and-take with his parents.

In following this procedure, Sarah found it very difficult to yield. She was blocked by shame, fear, guilt, anxieties, all of them increasingly painful as she began to remember. Certain words could not be uttered, and she could not bear to look at certain scenes again.

Her first memories of earliest childhood were of being in a bathtub with her brother. The memory was dim. She could not say with much exactness what actually happened. She could only recall a mixed-up feeling of excitement, pleasure and fear. She thought perhaps her brother had kicked her, but she wasn't sure. Sarah did remember, however, that her brother had something she didn't have, and the discovery was a shocking surprise. In fact, she recalled exploring and probing and trying to find deeper inside herself what her bother had on the outside of his body.

She recalled the enema bag her father was so free to use, especially with her brother. It was a nightly affair. Her brother would scream his protests, but the father would only tell the boy that he had had all day to move his bowels and if he didn't want an enema all he had to do was to take care of himself during the day. Sarah remembered her brother's screaming and howling vividly, while she related the memory. She, too, was given enemas by her father, but she did not resist as her brother did, knowing it would do no good.

She recalled once seeing her father in the nude, and experienced again the terrible fright and choking feeling when she saw his penis, an organ she expected to be no larger than her brother's. She had never seen her mother nude, but in her fantasy she was certain her mother had a penis, too, probably as large as her father's. Sarah felt that she was the only one in the whole world who was deprived of a penis.

Sarah told of waiting for her father to come out of the bathroom. He usually emerged while he was pulling his pants up or buttoning them. Indescribable excitement surged in her during the moments of expectancy, as her eyes stole furtive glances to see if she could catch a glimpse of his organ. She recalled the arguments between her father and mother at night, when he would beg the mother to let him come into her bed. Overhearing, it seemed to Sarah that her mother was defending herself against something unbearable the father was going to do to her. She thought her mother was being dirtied, insulted, that her father was offensive and disgusting to the mother, perhaps even injuring her.

Then, when her mother finally yielded, Sarah heard her father's animal-like sounds, rising in a crescendo to something that filled the child with strange, morbid feelings of terror and shame. She felt that her mother hated her father for doing these awful things to her, and she hated him, too, as though they were happening to her. When she went to bed at night, she recalled these memories over and over again, and hated her father more and more each time.

These experiences were much more shocking to Sarah than they would have been if she had enjoyed what all children need—a mother at home with her; a mother interested, caring and loving. If this had been the case, the results of listening to such a relationship would not have been so serious and lasting, although it would have been a traumatic experience. As it was, living in a desert-like world, Sarah did not develop according to the normal progression of children; as she grew into maturity, she did not advance along the lines of physical growth and ability, establishing more and more independence.

In the period between six and seven, she would have played with girls and related to them as more of an individual in her own right, without her mother. A little after her twelfth year, she would have begun trying out and testing attitudes toward boys, becoming acquainted with patterns and forms of heterosexual relationships. As she advanced in the physical and spatial sphere with new capacities, she would have risen to her current field of time with appropriate reactions and abilities. All of these functions would have enabled her to become independent of her mother.

Sarah met the young man who was to become her husband while she was still in high school. He helped her with her homework, carried her books for her, escorted her when she needed him, and took her to nice places. After graduation, they continued to "go steady." She felt safe with him, and he was always good to her. She could depend on him, and did so more and more. Happy in his arms, Sarah felt he was devoted to her, and when he kissed her she enjoyed it completely. But when he tried to become more aggressive in his love-making, something unpleasant happened to her. She shrank and became rigid, which stopped him from going any further until after they were married.

In their sexual relationship after marriage, Danny, her husband, was very careful and tender. He almost never hurt her, and she was pleased to cooperate with him whenever he wished, but she never had any sensations that might lead to an orgasm. Sexually she was frigid. Danny accepted her reaction as one of shyness, innocence and purity. He adored her.

A woman with Sarah's background could not have had a sexual life with a husband that did not contain disgusting implications—indeed, it was certain to be considered a dirty relationship, one fired with hatred. Yet Sarah insisted she never had a feeling of hate for her husband. Instead, she had regressed to the level of association called the oral-dependent receptive relationship, that is, the original form of relating that takes place between infant and mother. On this level, as the analyst knows, the husband comes to be a mother figure. Sarah did not hate Danny because he was not a heterosexual object; he was not a father surrogate. All her husband gave her physically, mentally and sexually, Sarah accepted as she had accepted milk and food from her mother in her first year of life.

Her mother's illness came after her marriage, so that in order to take care of the ailing woman Sarah had to bring her family to live with her parents. One can well believe that it was a most trying time. Her father constantly upset her mother by his crude attitudes. Sometimes he dropped a bottle of medicine, or his hand shook and spilled the medicine on the pillow. He accused the nurses of incompetence and bewailed the money it all was costing; he antagonized the doctors.

After her mother's death, Sarah's father became more of a problem than ever. He chose Danny to be his father-confessor. He would corner him and weep and explain himself, trying to justify the aggressions he had committed against his wife by dramatizing his own nervous state and his terrible unhappiness. Does anyone know what a husband feels? he would wail. Could anyone understand his grief at the loss of the one person in the world he loved the most? Danny was absorbed by all this. The wailing sessions became longer; before the evening was over, Danny would be exhausted by his father-in-law's emotional outbursts. But he had no defenses; he was trapped.

Sarah began to realize she was getting very little of her husband's company. She saw her father diverting her husband's interest from herself as he had done with her mother, and unconsciously she knew there was nothing he would not do to take from her anything or anyone she might have. As she felt Danny slipping away from her, she regressed to the old striving to find her mother. It was at this time that the colitis first attacked her.

Before the language that is made of words comes the language comprised of symbols, belonging more to fantasy and the dream; and before the words and symbols comes still another language: preverbal—the language of the body. Sarah now regressed to this level of gastrointestinal body language. In the earliest phases of development, adaptive mastery and living pleasure are confined to alimentary function. Survival depends solely on eating. The only source of food is the breast, and there is only one breast. If you do not have it, you die; if somebody else has it, you die. You have to battle for it in a grim and savage war in which you either kill or get killed. Everybody in the world is your rival, and the rival must be eliminated wherever possible.

In Sarah's deepest breast-seeking fantasies, the competitors had to be tackled with the first apparatus for adaptation she knew. Symbolically, in her unconscious fantasy, she had to swallow them to conquer them, and then destroy them within herself. In her dreams and fantasies, fierce struggles were waged. Her dream figures slashed each other to bits, tearing up the terrain which was the battleground—her intestines. In one dream she related, she killed the whole hospital staff. Her diarrhea attacks, which took place eighteen to twenty times a day, contained the actual blood and byproducts of the destructions that were taking place in her intestines.

The intestines have a special function in the general economy of the community that is the body. They digest and excrete. The brain has the special function of discharging emotions, symbolizing, thinking and making language for communication. When the intestines have to take over the function of the brain, they become over-taxed with responsibility and break down. This is the sub-symbolic and ultra-primitive life to which Sarah regressed. Symbolization is an advance. In fact, when Sarah was beginning to improve, my treatment rerouted the language from her intestines to the higher areas in her brain where symbols could be made and utilized for discharging functions so essential to the maintenance of the total organism's integrity.

At that point in the analysis, Sarah produced a dream in which, on the symbolic level, she disowned the intestinal condition. She dreamed that one of her boys was having diarrhea. Symbolically, then, Sarah was not the one who was having trouble. She had disowned the sickness, but not without having to dispose of it, in her dream, into the symbolic sphere of her son. The mechanism of projection and riddance of her condition, even though it was symbolic, had its effect upon her organism, proving that motivations of physical activity can originate in symbols.

When her diarrhea stopped, and physical success was attained in her cure, Sarah was able to carry on the function of intake, retention and riddance on the symbolic level. But now the analysis had to proceed until she could achieve the fourth cardinal feature of aliveness—reproductivity—meaning love and sexuality.

She began to achieve it one day, when she suddenly stopped speaking as she lay on the couch and could say nothing for several minutes. I suggested to her that when such blocking takes place, the fantasies she is not aware of consciously could very well be about her analyst. I suggested further that she should try to say whatever came into her mind at that time. She could report no ideas, but she was able to tell about a feeling she couldn't understand. At that moment, she said, she hated me. I asked her to describe the feelings, or any other feelings she might be having. There was a long pause, and then she added, "I also feel excited and afraid." I asked whether she remembered ever having such a combination of feelings at one time. Then she recalled the feelings of hatred she had for her father when she listened to his intercourse with her mother in the next room.

This was the first expression of her erotic transference—the masochistic wishes for the sadistic father's offenses, injuries and degradations. What she wanted unconsciously was to experience again, with her analyst, the excitement of the fantasies of her early childhood. In fact, she had already experienced this fantasy in her unconscious, but the only part of it that could achieve conscious awareness was the hatred.

The shame and guilt associated with such wishes force the patient to distort or disguise them, so that instead of wishing the analyst to make love to her she wishes him to punish, injure and degrade her. Then she hates him for fancied sadism. But basically she wants the analyst to make physical love to her, a desire which she expresses on this hate level (sado-masochistic), the only level she has ever known.

By this time our relatioiship was good enough so that I could interpret her hatred of me to her as an expression of sexual love and desire. Such interpretations are given to a patient with great scientific caution so that the patient experiences as little shame, guilt and anxiety as possible at these revelations of unconscious wishes. I explained her feelings to Sarah as the natural living outcome of our positive association on the mental level, now extending itself into the physical being where it had become a desire for physical contact and unification.

When such erotic stirrings occur, it is an indication that the patient is rising to higher levels of human relatedness. The urge to contact, combine, be mutual and coalesce with another, rather than be deflected from the other to separateness, is a sign of growing maturity. The fate of such impulses and strivings depends upon how they are dealt with in the analytical situation. Coarse handling could spoil the whole process of analysis. The analyst waits for just such a transference of feelings that have, in early life, been driven underground by the shocking actions of desexualized and frightened parents.

This is the time when the incubator that is the analysis can perform work of the highest complexity, which nature has failed to do. Instead of being ashamed of his wishes, the patient is encouraged to have them. Of course it also has to be made clear that the analytical situation is a professional one and precludes physical contact, but at the same time the patient is assured that there is no harm if the relationship continues in its loving way on the psychic and symbolic level.

As human beings, there is no reason why people cannot love each other in this way. It is a matter of one being creative and additive with the other. In Sarah's case, her love for her analyst had to be dealt with in two ways. She had to see it as the repetition of the old experience she had had with her father, which she fell to by temporal gravity, and then related to her analyst with the feelings she had for her father during her childhood. Secondly, she had to understand that her experience with her analyst was a new and different one.

She had to learn, further, how to distinguish the present from the past, to recognize the difference between one kind of relationship and another, between one kind of man and another. She came to know that a man did not have to be what her father and brother were. A man could be someone who had something to give, as did her husband. This knowledge could have come only from the experiences on the mental level that she went through with her analyst.

When Sarah began to feel the sexual stirrings for her analyst which had been latent on the mental level, they were extended into her physical being, which reflected them back again into the mind, reinforcing the fantasied impulses to such intensity that her desire broke through to consciousness. As the experience took place in her mind, it became known to her through the words that name the kind of feeling she was having. It is the words, and the names of feelings, that enable one to differentiate and discriminate between different experiences. Fortunately for Sarah, her husband was able to give a different kind of love and activity from her father, and she could now relate to him on a basis of respect, love and mutuality. Having overcome the devitalization of her symbolic mental sphere by achieving the fourth cardinal feature of aliveness through her relationship with her analyst, she now had the anti-gravity capacity to lift herself away from the past and live in the present.

In her analysis, Sarah learned other truths. She learned that self-preservation is the first law of nature, and that self-interest is a virtue. Her beginning was an unfortunate one, but it was nobody's fault. She couldn't even resent the circumstances, because they just happened to be what they were. That her mother was hungry for mothering and so necessarily had to deprive her, was something in the making for thousands of years of descendancy and inheritance. Not winning the love of her mother was no reflection on herself and didn't mean she was unworthy. When Sarah was finally convinced she couldn't get love out of her mother, who had none to give, her self-esteem no longer suffered.

Her greatest problem was her father, who continued to try aggressively to get from her what he had previously gotten from his wife, on the basis of the divine right of fatherhood. Sarah learned not to hate him, nor to judge him, but to defend herself against his insinuations, accusations and assumptions and not to fear them.

She became active and did for herself, and little by little, having gained initiative and self-respect, she became more able to give to others. With her new understanding, Sarah awakened sexually, and life took on color and meaning. Her two boys also became important to her for the obvious reason that they gave her the opportunity to live out natural womanhood and motherhood, both of which are roles as glorious as any human being could wish for.

Chapter 2

Amazon Wives

There is a symbolic truth in the old saying that marriages are made in heaven, for if heaven is a place to ascend to, then the body and dome of the womb, where the marriage is consummated, is indeed a heaven. From scientific investigation, however, we have learned that the real reason people marry is because of unconscious needs and strivings, of which they are completely unaware.

For example, a certain kind of neurotic marries because the mate fits his own neurosis. The known reasons for the marriage are simply veneer—more specifically, rationalizations. We define rationalization as a conscious realistic justification for the living and acting out of unconscious needs and motives beyond the awareness of the individual. Thus people marry each other to work out, and work through, the emotional tensions contained and bound up in housings which are the internalized experiences that took place between them and the outside world in early life. These experiences are repressed and pushed down under the surface of the mind, but they have a buoyancy of their own and keep pushing upward to emerge again.

Such reliving of old experiences is represented vividly in the case of a family which was the result of a marriage between two neuroses. The wife, Martha, came to me a little more than five years before the husband, Phillip, appeared. When I think of Martha in retrospect, she seems to me like a personification in reality of Coleridge's ancient mariner, with his desolate cry, "Water, water everywhere, and not a drop to drink." For Martha had everything reasonably necessary for a human to achieve satisfaction and gratification —a husband, a home, a son, a pleasant community to live in—yet she was starved for love, hungry for association, and unable to utilize her realities. She was afraid she would die, and lived as though she were destitute of all the good things available to her.

The expression on Martha's face was like that of a hungry infant watching its mother leave the room without giving it food—depressed, forlorn, helpless and unhappy. Her chief complaint was depression. Life had lost its appeal, she said. Her outlook was pessimistic, and she declared she didn't know what she was living for. This condition had existed for years, and she wondered whether it would ever end. She got up in the morning with a feeling of heaviness and despair which she felt powerless to overcome. Now and then she took a short nap and the feeling disappeared, but the bright and cheery periods which followed were short and infrequent.

Martha traced her sickness back to the dismal experience of spending the first two years of her marriage with her husband's family, in which he was an only child. She herself appeared constitutionally able to stand many rigors, a robust, handsomely constructed female who nevertheless had that beaten look on her face. Her parents were poor and underprivileged immigrants. The father was a solemn, silent, brooding man. He was inarticulate but he was able to make it clear that he intended no one should bypass him; he was the dominant figure in his world. His wife, Martha's mother, was a cringing, suppliant, overworked, martyrish lummox of a woman who labored constantly to appease and supply her three sons, and at a time too early called on Martha, her only daughter, to share her labors.

Martha hated the female role. She envied the male his masculinity, privileges and prowess, and vowed in her inner soul that she would escape the *sturm und drang,* the perpetual self-sacrifice of her mother's life. The opportunity to do so came, so she thought, when she went to work as a stenographer in an accounting firm headed by her future husband, Phillip. She was flattered and thrilled when he seemed attracted to her, believing it scarcely possible that such a man should want her. Later, however, she was aware that he possessed moods and attitudes she found repellent, and she resisted the idea of marriage to him.

Before marriage they had sexual intercourse in which he was the directed and helped one. He gave her the seductive lie that it was his first sexual experience and seldom missed the opportunity to inform her, facetiously, that she had taken his virginity. When she told him of her reluctance to marry him, his entreaties became frantic and pathetic. "I finally yielded," she told me, "when he sent in an envelope a lock of blond curly hair that he had stolen from his mother's jewel box. It was hair she had shorn from his long curls when he was six years old."

In spite of her reluctance, there were strong inducements that ultimately brought Martha to this marriage. It meant the achievement of two ambitions. One was the conscious wish to be a member of a high-class American family. The other, an unconscious wish, was to attain the masculine identification which Phillip was offering her on a silver platter. Then, too, there was the beautiful home he lived in, itself an added attraction when he suggested that they live with his parents. In her fantasies, she was the daughter of these elegant people; she dreamed of accompanying her mother-in-law to teas and parties and fancied herself introduced as the beloved daughter-in-law.

Phillip, in brief, was a trap for her. He appeared to offer a dream home, with wealthy and cultured parents; a little boy she could make into a man, with whom she could identify, and thus achieve her longed-for role in life. She could not know that her unconscious aspirations toward masculinity would lead her into a blind alley from which she might never have returned.

In spite of the lower social standing of Martha's people, Phillip's family raised no objections to the marriage. The father was a gentleman, mild, rather unnoticed, always ready with euphemisms, banal ideas, or submissive and appeasing attitudes. The mother was an attractive, high-spirited, charming and ingratiating person, with many friends and admirers.

In her mother-in-law's home, Martha came to feel almost at once what children of mothers who are infantile, possessive and competitive feel—the wordless, subtly expressed attitudes in pantomime that imply: This is my house, and all that is in it is mine, mine, and mine alone, and not yours. You are here on my sufferance. . . . Do as I say when I order it. . . . Wait until I want you, and when I don't want you, keep away.

Such attitudes, of course, relegated Martha to a secondary position and deprived her of initiative and dignity. The feelings of inferiority she had always suffered because of her lowly background now reached serious dimensions, and her fantasy of being the mother-in-law's darling daughter was rudely shattered. In a hundred subtle ways the older woman made Martha feel low and unworthy. She was particularly scornful at the very times she was most effusive with her friends, and as Martha became more depressed the mother-in-law seemed to become more animated. Naturally life with Phillip's family became a nightmare for Martha.

For all that Phillip's mother was charming, well-groomed and socially sophisticated, beneath this façade she was an exhibitionist, shallow and empty, jealous of her position and possessions, desexualized, hating men, unable really to enjoy life or permit anyone else to do so. When Martha complained to her husband about how his mother belittled her, Phillip refused to see it and sided with his mother, just as he denied that his mother belittled him and degraded him by comparing him unfavorably with others, making snide remarks about his inefficiencies and incapacities.

The fact was that although Phillip was the "spared" one after his marriage, he had not been so fortunate before that event. By tacit agreement between his mother and father, he had been the "sacrificial lamb," whom his mother dominated, belittled and ridiculed, demolishing every opinion he had. After his marriage, she transferred this discharge to Martha. It is doubtful whether Phillip would ever have married Martha if he hadn't seen in her a good possibility of achieving for himself a disposal area so that he might avoid the perfidious activities of his destructive mother, as his father had avoided them by using him. Consequently he stood by and watched his mother destroying his wife as she had destroyed him, not only without interfering, but consciously denying what was happening.

Martha found herself excluded more and more from the activities in the house. She had no one to confide in, nobody with whom to express the terrible frustration she was experiencing. To the outside world she had made a fine match, far above her station. She was living in a beautiful home, but only Martha knew that in this house she was degraded and shunned.

Her sex life with Phillip was characterized by her vigorous activities toward him. He was yielding and cringing, and she directed him during the sex act, like a director advising an actor what to do. He waited to be asked or to be told. The initiation of the act never came from him. She prided herself on her own potency and passionate nature, and remarked about how frequently she could engage in intercourse. Phillip was compliant and submissive, and happy to be so.

In one of her analytic sessions, Martha said: "I was waiting for my husband to come home, to take him in my arms and love him."

"You sound as though you were a big man talking about your little wife," I remarked.

"I don't see that at all," she answered, without humor.

Martha admitted never being satisfied or relaxed after intercourse, as was her husband. They never experienced simultaneous orgasm. She had to have a few orgasms first, and then he followed—a typical procedure in the sexual activity of people who live you-or-me lives.

It had been tacitly agreed in their romantic days, by the symbolic gesture of the curls, that Phillip would be Martha's "little girl," and thus she would achieve symbolically the role she craved. But there was a complication. Phillip's mother had seized this prize before Martha appeared on the scene, and she had no intention of handing it over to Martha, who was no match for her in the struggle between these two pseudo-sperm figures.

You might ask why Martha could not be a real "man" who would fight against such a predatory, aggressive person as her mother-in-law. The answer is that in this house, the arena where the two Amazons fought a grim battle for the prize, Phillip, all the cards were in the mother's hands, and Martha could not compete with this lioness who was the original predator. In the beating she took, Martha had become the archaic alternate in terms of mood and temperament. As her mother-in-law's elation increased, so did Martha's depression.

The figures of early life are internalized and identified with, and of these figures the one who is the dominant and most frightening can become the self. Consequently, when Martha was called upon to defend herself against this woman, she found the failures of her family constellation repeated. The previously internalized father image was the one who was living his life out through her, and he was no match for the wily, clever, divisive mother of Phillip. Like him, Martha retreated within herself to brood and become depressed.

Though she was beaten, bedraggled and forced to crawl away, Martha still had her husband, by virtue of the social and religious rites of the marriage contract; but by the time they moved into their own home, her mental sickness had reached such magnitude that two years of treatment with me could not pull her out of her depleted state. She remained so depressed and suicidal that I called for a consultation with two other psychiatrists, and we agreed she should be hospitalized for custodial care. But neither Martha nor Phillip accepted this verdict. They decided to make a go of things as well as they could.

Three-and-a-half years after Martha's unsuccessful treatment ended, her husband came to me for analysis. He told me he did not consider his wife's treatment a failure; on the contrary, he felt she had been helped to a considerable extent. But Phillip himself was now so mentally sick as to be not too far away from an institution.

As his analysis progressed, it appeared that Martha had won back much of the ground she had lost. She had been able to recover a sufficient amount of her own strength to relieve herself more and more of the plague of Phillip's fate, of being degraded and humiliated. As she became relieved, however, Phillip once again had to take back his original sickness. More and more Martha had restricted his life. He was cut off from all his friends; he rarely saw his parents.

Martha, in fact, was becoming progressively more demanding and tyrannical. She had learned to use her sickness as power, and she instrumentalized it to master her predator. Her depression, her headaches, the "fog that covers my brain," as she put it, and her outbursts of rage at the slightest disorderliness had Phillip walking a chalkline of obedience. The minutiae of their lives had become the dominant issues.

In all this, Martha was getting revenge on her husband for his former callousness in letting her "relieve" him of his mother's destructiveness. She had become the sadistic brute, and he again the masochistic female. Her unconscious plan, the strategy she now used to survive, was to isolate Phillip as he had previously isolated her in his mother's house.

Martha demanded that he come home for dinner at a specified time, otherwise the work of the house could not be finished. As a result, he could not engage in any activity that might possibly involve him in any irregularity of hours. His scope of operations was now narrowed down to where reality activity was at a minimum. Using some rationalization, he maneuvered himself out of the firm of accountants in which he was a partner and became one of the salaried employees. He confined himself, moreover, to a specific department in which he would have no contentious or bargaining relationships with anyone. He had to do this because of the aggressive tendencies that resulted from mounting anxiety and tensions within him.

Their five-year-old boy was an overactive, daring and reckless child who dominated the household, including Martha, with the same tyranny with which Martha dominated Phillip. This situation was a reductio ad absurdum. Phillip was made to be smaller than Martha, but, in order to make him even smaller, Martha made the proportions greater by making herself smaller than their five-year-old child. Only the unconscious could be capable of such tactics.

Phillip, however, had defenses and his own means of escape. They were the ones the infant resorted to when his mother was not yet present. He could use memory images and stimuli, out of which he could reshape reality and fantasy a life in which the wish for gratifying and satisfying experiences would be fulfilled.

By this time, he had reached the point where his only associations were those about whom he could fantasy in subways and buses, or when other drivers on the road kept trying to get ahead of him and cut him off. His romantic excursions into fancied situations with women on buses were beginning to frighten him because of the impulses that were threatening to be acted out with them and the anticipated consequences. His fantasies were also making such extensive inroads into reality that too much reality was being displaced. His adjustment to reality was becoming so tenuous that on occasion he would lose it altogether.

For example, when he was having intercourse with Martha, he would sometimes imagine he was with some young woman he had seen on the bus, and for a moment his state of mind would be such that he was not certain what woman he was actually with. That terrified him, quite naturally.

Unquestionably the three people in this family were engaged in macabre activities, but knowing what we do about the character of the sperm—its alternatives of do-or-die, to-be or not-to-be, him-or-me—it should not be surprising, nor should we be shocked at the grim warfare being waged by these mates and their offspring.

Although the struggle may not be as fierce in most homes, I venture to say it is not essentially too dissimilar in the families of our society today, where the mates live competitively with each other.

What we came to know about this family would never be discernible by casual examination, any more than an individual would be able to see the germs about us without the aid of a microscope. Phillip was a well-groomed, affable gentleman, rather shy, over-courteous. Martha was neatly attired and deferential with people. Closer inspection, however, would show both these people to be tense and over-alerted for what might be happening next. The tension could be interpreted as a readiness for immediate escape from a dangerous situation. These manifestations would not be obvious to the layman, because they are difficult to detect, and they are so prevalent in our culture today as to be inconspicuous.

Needless to say, there was no love or sexuality, reproductivity, or self-perpetuity in this home. Living took place on the gastro-intestinal level of who was going to eat up, macerate, digest, disintegrate, degrade and get rid of whom, who was going to be the "he" and who would be the "she" of the family.

Phillip was not a completely lost human being. There were positive influences in his life, too. His father, fortunately for him, was not the utterly beaten man Phillip's mother would have had him. Once the father took his son to a whorehouse, and although it was a sickening experience because father exposed son to the degrading position of letting him have intercourse with the same whore he had taken first, at least the older man could say: "This is how we men whose masculinity is assassinated and who are emasculated by our women—this is how we rebel and go elsewhere to buy an amount of life that can reinstate us to the biological position we should have."

The morbidity of such an experience could be analyzed on its own account, with all its intricate and complex implications, but that is not within the scope of this study. Let it be said, however, that it was better for both these men to have such an experience than to acquiesce and submit to the murderous despot who would do in their manliness completely. It was better than as though there were no rebellion at all.

Phillip had retained enough of this nonsurrender and defiance to wage a war in behalf of his own sexual realizations. It was a last bit of strength that caused him to seek professional help. Enough reality remained to impel him to do so. When he came to see me, he was well on his way to an institution, where he would have defeated his wife and son by achieving for himself the good mother that the hospital would be to him. Coming to me was implicitly a request that I save him from this final unreal and empty victory.

During his analysis, Phillip's early environmental, infantile deprivations, frustrations and injuries had to be lived over and over again for the sake of overcoming them. Later, he told of Martha's temper tantrums whenever he made a misstep. She pounded at him with her fists and pushed him around, threw things at him and used violent language. It was pointed out to him that this was a reversal of what is customary in our culture; the wife is not usually the brutal one. It is undesirable, of course, that anyone be primitive or brutal, but it is the lesser evil when the man is the brute.

Thus the first change that had to take place in Phillip was a basic shift in attitudes. He was made to see that as long as his wife initiated the activity and he remained the passive one, letting her have her way with him, he could never achieve his full mental strength. Gradually, he began to use her tactics. When she told him to "go to hell," he told her to "drop dead." When she pushed him around, he pushed her harder. This new relationship was shocking to Martha and jolted her into coming to see me a year after Phillip had started his analysis. Though she now had a justifiable complaint about his brutality, I was gratified because her suffering was now due to reality, whereas her previous depressions had been deep in her unconscious.

But Phillip and Martha had reached a low point. Both were now threatened, and neither had any place to go if they separated. They were locked in commitments, reinforced by the child. It had become a matter of all or none for them. Was there a way out?

They looked to me with despair, discouragement, pessimism. Phillip asked me if I thought there was any hope. I could see plenty of oases in this desert of their lives. They could be cultivated and thus caused to spread and overtake the sterile areas. Consequently, Martha returned for a continuation of her work with me, and then each one was in analysis with me concurrently.

Through therapy, Phillip's expanded and vitalized ego began to see that Martha had been his prey in the same manner that he had been the prey of his mother and father. He had enjoyed a period of peace by offering Martha's symbol systems to his mother for her psychic riddances, thereby saving himself. The reason Martha could not recover from her depression, even after they left his mother's house, was that Phillip had a stranglehold on her and would not let her achieve a position of self-esteem because that would automatically cause him to lose his, which he had gained at her expense. Martha had revolted, and as she gained strength had turned the tables on him and driven him back to his original position of being the degraded and humiliated one. Now that he was the underdog, he began to feel guilty for what he had done to her and became more honestly sympathetic and altruistic towards her. They had both been victimized by the pull of gravity in the temporal universe, in their preconceptual and elementary solitary strivings.

Phillip had suffered enough, and had gained enough surcease from his own degradations during the time Martha had relieved him by becoming his mother's whipping boy, so that he could now generate enough vitality for mutual striving with his wife and his analyst. Because of the analysis, he was capable of intercepting unconscious motivations. He saw that he did not need to continue to be feminine, passive and masochistic. He could shift to active masculine attitudes, and when he began to do so Martha also began to readapt.

I must pay tribute to these two patients for their tenacity, perseverance, trust and bravery. These qualities enabled them to continue to strive for what they were entitled to have by God and nature, a realistic span of life. They were the ones who climbed the mountain; I was merely the guide and sympathizer who accompanied them, but not without being significantly involved in their terrible emotional crises through the difficult and jagged terrain that had to be traversed.

When Phillip married Martha, it was, in a sense, as it is in all marriages, a family marrying a family. The families of both were going to be reconstructed for the purpose of overcoming what had offended, injured and threatened the security and survival of the respective mates in the early days of their lives. Phillip's punishing, depriving, rejecting, desexualizing mother had been internalized by him by way of overcoming the threat she was to him. This incorporated, repressed object figure within him was constantly striving towards externalization. His tendency was to find somebody to whom he could do what his mother had done to him to keep him inferior.

Martha's father, too, was externalized, living out his moody depression through her, but we must mention that there was also in Martha an introjected mother-figure who martyred herself for her sons and husband. When the situation called for the expression of this martyred mother's identification, Phillip's purposes were served —that is, Martha freely martyred herself for Phillip and his mother. That was when Martha was on the way to becoming the masochistically destroyed one.

What had more than anything else to do with Martha's collapse and morbidity was Phillip's mother's elaborate testament that all the world was her witness that she was wonderful, sweet, grand, delightful, darling. Martha had never met a person who did not say emphatically that her mother-in-law was a wonderful, sweet woman. In the face of such overwhelming evidence, Martha was convinced in her unconscious mind, as well as in her consciousness, that it was she who was no good, inferior, worthless. No wonder she thought, "I might as well be dead."

But Martha was able to see now that such a vast proselytizing on her mother-in-law's part, to cause so many people to make such flattering remarks about her, must have been the result of prodigious enterprise. These friends must have been appealed to in subtle ways, pandered to, and very likely threatened. Phillip's mother could only have been building a defense against a vicious crime that was being committed—building defenses and denials that would be commensurate with the enormity of the crime itself.

Until the realization that Phillip's mother was the devil incarnate, Martha never thought in her self-appraisal that *she* could be the good one. But as she began to understand how her mother-in-law was able to debilitate her, to understand the forces that caused Phillip unconsciously to permit his mother to do so, and how it was also that she had let it happen to her, Martha's depression lifted.

After a good deal of travail that was not without daring, even gambling, these people and their child achieved positions of dignity and good enough amounts of mutuality, earned for themselves, so that they were able to live their lives more harmoniously and hopefully.

Chapter 3

Crime Out of Guilt

A new and novel cure for enuresis (bed-wetting) has recently been advertised in newspapers and magazines, offering an unorthodox and unprofessional relief from this obstinate condition, long a discouraging problem to pediatricians, which persists in some children until the age of fifteen and occasionally for life.

The cure is a mechanical device which sets off a trigger when the child begins to wet. Bells ring, a gong sounds, a siren wails, lights glare and a spotlight is focused on the child. The child is fully awakened and startled, of course, although probably not too seriously shocked.

Whatever the curative effect, the mental mechanisms set into action by these alarms are pertinent and worthy of examination. We have found in treating children for enuresis that the problem is not only with the child but with the mother. When the child begins to improve, the mother (beyond her awareness) becomes the source of increased resistance to the child's cure. Deeper analysis discloses that, on the unconscious level, mother and child are both engaged in this primitive, instinctual activity, but the mother proclaims her righteous indignation and protests loudly. She admonishes, pleads, scolds and punishes, while the child experiences the shame. The transaction is a completely private one, secret and exclusive. I know, for instance, of a father who remained unaware his daughter wet the bed until she was thirteen years old. It was a secret the mother never shared with her husband.

What this means in the perspective of our examination is that the shame the mother had in her unconscious mind, for one reason or another, had to be disposed of, and the only way she could do it was to transmit it into the symbol formation of her child, who would never dare, or have the motive power, to stand up and say to the mother, "What are you doing to me?" The mother, because of her rationalized and conscious innocence, would deny everything, beat the child down, and render it helpless.

Now we can understand why the mechanical cure for bed-wetting works. When the bells ring and the gong sounds and the siren blows and the lights go on, it creates the feeling within child and mother that the situation is being broadcast. All the world is now in on the secret. The mother can no longer enjoy the vicarious pleasure of releasing her impulses through the child's activity. The bed-wetting ceases as soon as it is no longer a secret transaction, the child does not have to live out the shame which rightfully belongs to the mother, and the child is permitted to evolve beyond this infantile phase.

The mother experiences the pleasure of ridding herself of shame by seeing her child experience it in wetting, but it is not a solitary gratification. The exchange is on an instinctual basis and is therefore pleasurable to both, an example of the projection of effects— emotions such as guilt or anxiety.

It is not within the scope of this book to describe how the idea evolves in the child's mind that it is wonderful and marvelous to be participating in intimate activity with its parent, whatever the activity may be, pleasurable or painful. It all belongs to the instinctual stream, so it is wanted by the child as life itself. Thus a child can be employed by the parent to act out impulses the parent would like to act out but cannot and dare not. Further, the child will carry the shame, guilts and anxieties that are the invariable concomitants of the parent's infantile, instinctual activities or fantasies.

This was the situation in the life of a 15-year-old boy, Charles, who became a juvenile delinquent. His lawbreaking activity clearly proves that crime may be caused by guilt, rather than the commonly accepted reverse.

There was no sense in Charles' gesture when he smashed a jewelry store window, for no more reason than to be caught doing so. Not too far away was a police car which, consciously or unconsciously, he feigned not to have seen. I anticipated the delinquency of this adolescent, and indeed had predicted it to the father in the course of treating him during the previous year. But he had reacted to the prediction with skepticism and a defensive lack of understanding.

To understand how a state of mind is created that finally breaks out in a rash of criminality, present for all to see, we must go back to the experiential past and trace the red thread of the individual's life to the breakthrough. Then, and only then, can we really come to know what makes a criminal have to do what he does.

In the case of Charles, we begin with the marriage of the boy's parents. It was a marriage that could scarcely hold much promise for any family deriving from it. George and Thelma married because they were sexually compatible, but their sexuality was extremely infantile in nature. They engaged in it only when both were sufficiently anesthetized by alcohol to put to sleep the shame, anxiety and guilt that otherwise would have inhibited and blocked the releases.

They carried on an affair for a year before they were married. It was a year of indulgences in which each developed a powerful need of the other. Bound by their common guilt, each was prevented from becoming interested in anyone else, and consequently, to use George's expression, there was nothing for them to do but "get spliced."

In the marriage, any differences that arose between them were not allowed to go very far, nor were they ever talked out. George and Thelma simply had a few drinks and settled their problems in bed. The solution to their difficulties was a drowning in the deep sea of their orgies.

Before Charles was born, there was a great deal of going out. Dancing was the pastime they enjoyed most, and they frequently won first prize in contests. Their conversation was sparse and vague. Both exercised considerable caution to avoid words or ideas that might lead to controversial subjects—like why his parents had arrived without phoning first, or why her mother talked about no one but herself. Their friends were also dance enthusiasts, and when they didn't dance they played cards. George and Thelma's intellectual relationships with these other people were as shallow as their own. Aside from card-playing and dancing, conversation extended only to eating places and which restaurants specialized in what dishes.

When Thelma was pregnant, both she and George resented it. There was no dressing up, no dancing. They were too restless and irritable to play in a game without getting into an argument, in which tempers would rise to a shrill pitch. They simply endured each other through long hours of boredom and silent hatred.

George was himself the son of exploiting parents, and the target of a jealous older sister who was four years his senior and had certainly not welcomed his arrival. His mother was the doting, overconscientious, overprotective type who puts on a sweater over a sweater and always contrives to shove another spoonful of food into an offspring's mouth when he is already stuffed. She supplied George with an actual bottle and nipple until he was ten years old and after that kept feeding him candies and cookies frequently during the day. When he was playing with his friends (surprisingly he was a fairly good athlete), he would sneak away from them and meet his mother behind the stairs of the tenement where they lived, and there she slipped him his "bottle." George was never without a sense of terror that one of the other children would find this out.

Such extreme babying and overprotection alternated with disloyalty and underprotection when disputes or harangues occurred between George and his father. At these times, the mother invariably sided with the father. In spite of his mother's destructive, infantilizing attitude, it was his brutal father with whom George identified. That gave him just enough strength and stamina to overcome his passive, receptive tendencies and enable him to make himself into a professional man. He became a successful practicing dentist, retaining the interest in athletics he had had as a boy. After Thelma gave birth to a son, he continued his activities as a scoutmaster.

George's general demeanor could be described as "sweet." He was sweet to the boys, to his patients, to his many friends. The attention and interest he gave his son were on the basis of "children should be taken care of"—one should be considerate and kind to a child. In sports activities he bent over backward to be fair to the other children, thus proving his own sportsmanship. His impartiality extended itself to his relationship with Thelma. He was nice to her because "women are lovely."

But the impartiality upon which George prided himself was neither appreciated nor enjoyed by his wife and son. To them he was not aware of their existence in the special way that a wife and son would expect. Actually the nondistinction they sensed could be equated with their extinction. Wife and son felt that they were not personalized by him but instead were lost in a generalization, and thus didn't mean anything to him. His sweetness to others, as far as they were concerned, was the insult added to injury.

The reason, of course, that George disregarded his wife and son was that he wanted to disown being the disregarded one, the feeling he had experienced at the hands of his parents in childhood. His father not only had administered physical beatings, but he had a chronic disposition to refute, oppose and negate every idea or contention his son expressed. George not only had developed a tremendous hatred for his father, but he had no trust or confidence in his mother.

We have said that a neurosis marries a neurosis, and a family marries a family. Thelma would never have married George, who did not particularize her, if she could have done anything more than generalize him. She was a slim, attractive, smart-looking young woman who before her marriage had many boy friends. She classified them according to their ability to dance, and, equally important, where they took her and how they dressed. Her involvement with George was more a matter of propinquity and circumstance than conscious choice. They had met at a party which happened to split up so that she was thrown with George. Because she enjoyed her new friend's dancing, she dropped the man she had come with and wound up with George in his office, on the couch in his waiting room. She enjoyed his advances but allowed him no actual love-making the first time. Next night they went dancing again, and that night they had sexual intercourse on George's couch. That was where all their dates ended, from the second night onward.

Crime Out of Guilt

Thelma's family of orientation consisted of four sisters and her parents. Her father was a man of affairs, a great doer in his clubs, business and musical groups. In Thelma's home, there was outward harmony but a lack of vivacity and color in the interchanges between family members. The father was nearly always absent, not only because he wanted to keep away but because he was driven out by being unwanted in this society of females. There was an unspoken resentment between Thelma's parents. Her father covertly blamed his wife for not providing him with a son, feeling that this was her way of impugning his virility. The mother blamed her husband for not being strong enough to provide her with a boy for her own having and keeping.

Thelma had two dominant drives. Because of her identification with her mother, one was to keep every man at a distance, to get him out of the way. The other was to depict every man as someone to get revenge on for her own nondignification and noncomplementation by her father. George meant as little to her as she meant to him. That left their son with parents who had no love for each other and, as Charles felt, no love for him.

Not having been complemented by her father or her husband, Thelma had necessarily gravitated to her preconceptual, elemental, spermatic identification, and to achieve her masculinity on the symbolic level she exploited Charles for that purpose. There was, of course, no interference from her husband. In reality, Charles was a field of enterprise and exploitation for both parents.

As children always are at an early age, Charles was aware of these facts without understanding them. Oddly, it is not until later life that people, through the unconscious mechanism of repression and denial, become unable to know consciously what they know unconsciously somewhere within themselves. But Charles' knowledge was of no use to him, because he had no access to weapons of defense; these were allotted to his parents by the social order. Consequently, as the infant develops hate as a source of relief for himself, Charles hated and feared society, as he did his parents.

The juvenile delinquent hates his parents in order to force love, and he hates society for the same reason. He is also like the infant who has not had the chance to develop anything to give to society so that society is willing to give something back, so he becomes an aggressor, attempting to take by force what he is not entitled to in the ordinary course of events.

There were, too, natural forces surging within Charles—forces that antedated his immediate forebears by many years. They were the forces that urged him to be a man, to do, live and create. But these forces had to remain primitive, diffuse, unspecialized and unchanneled. They could not mesh with any kind of order and be integrated, but instead remained locked up within him, threatening to burst out at any time in some senseless way.

My acquaintance with this situation began shortly after the death of Thelma's father. George was referred to me by his family physician because of an alarming change he had noticed in his patient's personality. Further, in the month before his appointment with me, George had become sexually impotent. He complained of apathy, spotty loss of memory, and a growing indifference to his work. Now and then he would be overtaken by a strange feeling of fear, not knowing what he feared.

In other respects, the only change in his life was that his wife visited her mother more frequently, and that where once all her sisters and their husbands and families had been his patients, they had now switched to other dentists, and there were veiled allusions to the poor dentistry he had done on them.

The explanation of George's situation could be found only in the analytical work which enables us to look into the activities of the unconscious mind. One of the ways we gain access to it is through the patient's dreams. In his first dream, always a significant one in the analytic process, George was having a session with me when his wife entered the room, took out a gun and shot me.

The meaning of that pantomime would vary on different levels of unconsciousness, and its deepest meanings do not concern us here. On the face of it, however, it meant that something had happened to me in George's dream that might otherwise have happened to him. The wish fulfillment was that what happened to me at the hands of Thelma, therefore, did not happen to him.

On the unconscious level, the theory is that for every effect there is a cause, and, in George's unconscious mind, if Thelma's father died, something had caused it. Who else could cause it but those to whom he was related, his wife and daughters? George anticipated that what had happened to his father-in-law could happen to him; he could be next on the list of those who were gotten out of the way. That Thelma's family deserted him en masse as patients, and she absented herself so much more, reinforced his suspicions. In order to escape this danger, which he could not consciously define, he developed avoidance tendencies and withdrew more and more from people and interests.

On the unconscious level, George's suspicions were justified, because Thelma's mother, since the loss of her husband, had to find another male mind through whose symbol systems she could deprive the owner of his masculinity, and in which she could find a disposal area to rid herself of what was unwanted. George, whom she liked least of her sons-in-law, was the logical candidate for this exploitation.

Thelma's own exploiting of George, not unlike her mother's, had been mild compared to what it became after her father's death, when her mother began to put pressure on her by constantly alluding to George's faults, shortcomings and weaknesses. George was, indeed, now severely threatened. The stream of abuse he had been able to shunt off on Charles was becoming a flood that engulfed him. Looking back into his life, we can recall how one of his parents "ganged up" with the other at critical times to commit aggressions against him. Thus, through identifying with these aggressors, it was quite natural for him to gang up with his wife to step up his aggressions against his son. Even as in his dream he was glad to have the analyst shot instead of himself, he was willing to have Thelma turn her destructiveness towards Charles.

The attacks on Charles were becoming so great that his own aggressive impulses were being mobilized against his parents. Because of the terrible things Charles wanted to do to them in his fantasy, he unconsciously anticipated retribution in kind. He was not, it must be noted, a neglected child in the conventional sense.

He had his own room, his bicycle and sports equipment, and whatever other boys appeared to have. But there was a significant difference. Until he became the target of their aggressions, his parents had failed to specify him. They never called him "our boy" but "the boy," or else they talked about him impersonally.

As a matter of fact, no one in this family had personalized any other member. There was no spiritual relationship between them, no sympathy, no altruism, but merely a relationship in the physical sense. This was only a relative indifference, however. As we have seen, the parents were interested unconsciously in Charles' symbol systems as areas for disposal of unwanted feelings and concepts of themselves.

Charles' room was adjacent to that of his parents. They did not take the ordinary, sensible precautions to keep their adolescent son out of range of their sexual activity. Charles would be awakened during the night by the sounds from the next room. Although there was physical union between George and his wife, psychically they were as separate as strangers. Their respective fantasies were autistic (alone), since neither had the capacity to blend or be mutual on the symbolic level. It was as though each were doing unallowed, unsanctioned things about which they felt shame, guilt and anxiety. They had to eliminate these feelings by unconsciously arranging for Charles to peep and eavesdrop so that he would be the guilty and shamed one.

The stimulation and excitement overpowered Charles, so that he was driven to engage in scoptophilic (peeping) activities. These are partial sexual instincts, fragments of sexuality occurring in early childhood and thus ridden with associated anxiety, shame and guilt. To his feelings of guilt for his hatred of his parents, and his fear of punishment for the fantasied aggressions he acted out against them, Charles now had the added deep shame he felt over his fantasied participation in their sexual activities, fantasying himself through identification with one or the other in his auto-erotic activity.

If the parents had been really concerned about Charles, it would have been a simple matter for them to see that the door was not left ajar, as though they had forgotten, and the dim lights would not have been left on, enabling him to see. He could, indeed, have been placed in another room, but by giving him his opportunity to see and hear they were able unconsciously to have him assume their shame and guilt and thereby be free of it.

Because of her ability to disparage others, Thelma was the guiltless one in her own eyes, having won her mother's approval particularly. George, too, propitiated his friends and patients with a false affability and "sweetness" and expiated his guilt through his righteous services to the youngsters in his scout troop. Charles, then, was left with his guilt and shame, with no way of disposing of it. There was no one for him to turn to for love and approval, who would assure him he was good and wanted.

At the time George was stricken with sexual impotency, Charles was aware of it, overhearing George berate his wife as the cause. But because of primeval cause-and-effect theories and wishes, the boy felt that he was responsible for his father's plight because of the wish-fulfilling fantasied aggressions he had perpetrated on him. In this way, son had displaced father. The guilt of his parents, which he had taken to himself, overwhelmed the boy.

Guilt, however, is no more than an anticipation of punishment. Fear of the retribution that would overtake him oppressed Charles so unbearably that it had to be relieved. He had to have some kind of settlement, to know what his fate was going to be. It was better to know the punishment than to anticipate total annihilation, commensurate with the scope of his fantasied aggression toward his parents, and the shame and guilt that were crushing him. That was why he committed the crime of breaking the window. He thus worked out an economy for himself: he would be punished for this offense, instead of for the innumerable crimes that were occurring in his unconscious fantasy.

What further evidence do we have to prove the theory that the guilt caused the crime? At the time the window was broken, and the boy was taken to the police precinct station, the parents were called and the boy was released in their custody. They telephoned me and I arranged to see them in the next hour. It was a four-cornered session in my office. The father railed at the boy, accusing him, blaming him, threatening him, shouting unrestrainedly. The mother sat by, nodding and approving the father's condemnations. This went on for several minutes, and as it progressed Charles appeared more and more composed and complacent.

I interrupted finally and turned the tables, accusing the father and mother of failure in their responsibility to Charles and putting the blame directly on their shoulders. I reminded them that I had predicted they were going to have a juvenile delinquent on their hands if they did not change their attitude toward their son.

They remonstrated and defended themselves, but I was adamant and determined to prove them the guilty ones. While I was doing so, I watched Charles covertly to see what effect this was having on him. His expression became more and more strained, and finally he broke down in tears. I asked him what was the matter, and he choked out, "I feel so guilty and ashamed of myself."

"When did you start to feel this way?" I asked him.

"Just now," he sobbed.

What Charles wanted, of course, his father had been giving him —the punishment that expiated the guilt and shame in his unconscious mind. When I punished the father, the guilt and shame in Charles, not having been relieved, broke through to consciousness. Now the act of breaking the store window could be seen with conscious awareness of all its realistic meaning.

It was no longer part of his instinctual, unconscious, sexual fantasy, but had become a real situation which he had to face consciously.

It was this dramatic crisis in the lives of these three people that aroused them to the fact that their respective neuroses had to be dealt with seriously and rigorously, and by each, or else there would be no real position for them in a realistic society.

George was now capable of more direct inspection of his unconscious life, which was being lived by the internalized figures of his early childhood. Thelma, too, came to realize that what was preordained by her unfortunate father and mother was not what she had to live by. Through a more realistic understanding of what is normal, she could readjust and rearrange and reinterpret life and its meaning in her immediate time. Through analysis, these parents were made to realize that they had never related to each other in adult fashion, that their common denominators were elemental and each was in the service of relieving the other's infantile needs. Although they functioned on the same level, they did not complement each other as they would if they achieved their respective maturity.

Their sexuality was not love. It was the kind that pre-existed the levels of emotional maturity in which an individual is capable of sympathy and altruism. They came to know that there was a failure in development in each of them. The adults they might have become were still asleep. Relating to each other as retarded children, they were isolated from one another and suffered individually the invariable concomitants of infant love and sexuality—namely, shame, anxiety and guilt.

The most tragic fact about their lives was that they were using their only child to rid themselves of these emotions in the same way that their parents had used them. The only way they would not need to make a disposal area of their son's symbol systems would be if they could love maturely and thus be free from shame, anxiety and guilt.

Once George and Thelma were brought to the level of the present and placed on the path of understanding each other, they were able to see that they could live together altruistically and sympathetically. Then they were able to look at their son and see him as an individual who was the fruit of their union, and who gave them the opportunity to realize their own creativeness, and their own immortality, through him.

Chapter 4

The Matriarch

Marriage is usually the culmination of a series of elations, the heat of which joins the couple in the common idea of permanent bound-togetherness. The purposes served by these combinations are as numerous as the kinds of families evolving from them. Immature people marry for immature reasons, to state a truism, and mature people marry for mature reasons based on altruism, sympathy and the ability to combine with another person on higher levels of relationship. Such unions are uncommon in our time.

Fashions in courtship have changed radically in the four decades since the first World War. Women have become more active in the chase, doing the selecting, even the finding, and having their way. But when marriage brings together two people who lack anti-gravity capacity in the temporal universe and so fall back to their pre-conceptual elementary characteristics, and when the man offers an opportunity to his wife to achieve symbolic realization of her spermatic aspirations, the family becomes a matriarchy. The mother is now the head, the conqueror, the self-seeker, the "one and only," the one who disregards all others and whom none shall bypass. In such a family, deprivation and impoverishment of the children must necessarily be of a malignant nature, or so I have found.

To understand the implications of this reversal of roles, one might conceive of an impregnated ovum without a womb to nurture and warm and protect it, or of a newborn infant without a breast or its equivalent from which to get nourishment, and without the warm, soft, caressing hands of a mother.

Let us assume, for a moment, that the roles are reversed in fact. The father will serve as the mother and the woman as the man. How much femininity can a man really give, in the physical sense?

We see that he has rudimentary breasts, but how much milk and warmth can be obtained from those breasts? Now examine the rudimentary penis of a woman, her clitoris. How much of an ejaculation for creation can be obtained from this infantile organ? We do know, however, that the human being dreams, and in the dream there is no realistic limitation imposed upon the scope of a symbol or an idea. In the unconscious, as we have seen, the wish predominates, and in the hallucinating of the unconscious mind the clitoris can be fantasied as a great penis, and similarly a rudimentary nipple may be fantasied as an ample breast.

But as we also know, the dream and the fantasy, or the symbols of them, cannot be substituted for the actual physical realities of our lives. If we live off the symbolic substitute for the real thing, starvation and disintegration result. Thus the matriarch who presumes to be the man of the family, the creator, not only starves herself but starves her children and disintegrates them. She is a typical example of the very weak sperm who has to make the others weaker.

The much discussed "mom," meaning the kind of matriarch we have just described, exists when man is not capable of being a husband or father and walks out on his responsibility, leaving the woman to take on the job he has relinquished. It is a man's function to femininize his woman, and if he likes the vitality, then his wife will not only take over the role of the male but will get him out of the way.

A family of this kind came under my study some time ago. Bertram, the son of such a matriarch, came to me at the suggestion of a friend, after he had lost all hope. Later he told me that while he was on the way to my office he thought, Why should I go through this? It's too late. I might as well end it now and be relieved. It was all preordained and can't possibly be any different.

Bertram began his session with me by declaring: "I think you should give me shock treatment to knock some brains into my head, or maybe to knock my brains out." He smiled wryly, as though to say, I hope this pleases you, that I so invite you to use me for your own aggrandizement.

Though his smile was appealing, it masked a terrible hatred. I did not respond to his masochistic invitation, knowing it had nothing to do with me but related to the world of activities and relationships taking place inside himself. I merely waited for him to say something else that would merit a response. He had to give me something more real that related to me personally before we could begin an association.

Bertram asked me directly if I gave shock treatments. I told him I did not use this method of cure except on rare occasions, and explained that my special interest lay in helping to guide a person to know more about his life. I told him I had discovered from my experience that when people have put forth an effort to examine themselves directly they can know more about their lives and so be able to help themselves. Then I said, "Some day you will understand why you said I should knock brains in or out of your head; which to my way of thinking would be a most peculiar thing to do."

His question, however, was enough to enable me to make contact with his ego. I realized that this was a man who had never had the opportunity to do for himself nor possessed the psychic freedom to profit from such an opportunity.

Bertram's mother had two sons. He was the second-born. He never knew his father, whom the mother divorced when Bertram was two years old. The divorce gave the father no rights of visitation. The mother never remarried, although she was strikingly attractive. From his earliest recollections, Bertram considered his mother the most beautiful, and at the same time the most fierce, human being he had ever known. He feared and respected and worshipped her as a goddess. He never called her "mama." That name was reserved for Mollie, his nurse. He called his mother simply by that name.

Mother was not home very much. Her occupation as a high school physical training instructor kept her busy not only during the day but for after-school athletic activities. Mama, who had been with Mother before the birth of both of the boys, was Bertram's solace and haven. Harold, the older son, possessed Mother—or rather Mother possessed Harold completely. Bertram was referred to as his father's son. Mother called him Bert, or infrequently Bertie, but she always referred to Harold as "Boy" or "my boy." There was no doubt whom Mother preferred and loved and whom she rejected and hated. She made no bones about it.

This division of emotions—that is, allocation of love and hate—was so clear and definite that battles arose over it between mama and Mother. Frequently they approached the stage of violence. But in spite of the greater privileges accorded Harold, and the denials and deprivations Bert suffered, he loved and worshipped his brother, who was never unkind to him.

When Bert was thirteen years old, he began suffering from various ailments that were diagnosed as hypochondriacal. He had headaches, nausea and vomiting, occasional diarrhea and fears of heart disease. In spite of his frequent illnesses, he worked hard at his studies and was considered one of the brighter students in his class. When he graduated from high school, however, he was not able to attend his graduation exercises as he had never been able to win in any sports event. He had always managed to let his opponent win by acquiring some imaginary illness at the crucial moment. The same thing happened now. Mother had to send Harold for Bert's diploma.

When Bert was eighteen, mama committed suicide. Her act followed one of the violent scenes in which mama accused Mother of cruelty. The quarrel rose out of a situation in which mama had neglected to attend to a trivial matter that concerned Harold. During the argument that followed, mama accused Mother of having ruined her life by interfering with her marriage to the man she loved, thus depriving her own daughter of a legal father. However, the shock of standing up to Mother, after such a long and inclusive intimacy, was too much for mama, and she flung herself out of the window.

After this, Mother invited Doris, mama's daughter, who was now twenty, to come and live with them and take mama's place. Mother paid her a salary to manage the house. Doris' relationship with Mother was distant, guarded and suspicious, but obedient. Doris became interested in Bert in the same way mama had, although she was secretly in love with Harold, who was aloof and disdainful of her.

Bert inwardly resented and feared Mother, but he was completely dominated by her. She wanted him to be successful in business to secure a place for Harold. Although she loved Harold and gave him all the adulation and devotion of which she was capable, she let both him and Bert know that he was weak and would never be able to take care of himself. Because of essential identification with his mother, Bert had all of her feelings for his brother. In our sessions he talked frequently about his brother's lovable traits, his handsomeness.

Harold accepted his brother's adulation, but he did not respond with gratitude, nor even an attempt to justify the interest and devotion his brother showered on him. His was the position of being loved by divine right, of being the unawakened baby who was kept asleep by never being allowed to be hungry or uncomfortable so that he would wake up and strive in behalf of a conscious life. Harold could only take, digest and disintegrate. He could never create, nor was he able to give back.

More and more Bert came to belong to Doris, who still lived in their home. She sympathized with his fancied ailments, anxieties and nervousness. Bert believed that the devotion and affection he got from Doris was the same thing he had received from mama, but this was not true. Doris wanted Bertram because she couldn't get Harold, and she learned from Mother's manipulating, controlling, matriarchal ways that a man could be handled and managed, taken care of, done with and to as one wished.

Bert's shyness and modesty with girls was known and talked about. Harold had dates, but Bert was usually engaged in work that he brought home from his place of employment. Doris took every opportunity to knock on his door and ask him if there was something she could bring him. One evening, as she served him a glass of milk and some cookies, Doris bent down to place the tray on the night table and her dressing gown slipped open, revealing her complete nudity. It was a shocking experience for Bert. He said he thought his heart would leap out of his body, and he could scarcely breathe. Doris, he remembered, was not flustered at all. She merely pulled the robe together and tied the sash more securely. As she was about to leave his room, she ran her hand up the back of his neck and through his hair.

He could not put the experience out of his mind. "I got a feeling that I hadn't experienced for many years," he told me. "I had known it once when I was about four or five years old when mama was tender to me. I didn't fool myself that Doris was lovely, especially since Harold had talked about the coarseness of her features, and how she behaved like a housemaid. But her features, her hair, the way she walked, all combined themselves into something satisfying to think about."

After that evening, Bert said, he would wait for her to knock on his door. In fact, he would leave the door slightly ajar. Expecting her became so filled with anxiety and excitement, grew to be such a driving force within him, that he would feel dizzy and weak. When she finally appeared, he would sometimes be too much upset to say anything or do anything. The excitement culminated in symptoms of headache, or cramps, or pains around his heart. Of course Doris brought him aspirin and sympathized with him and nursed him. She even arranged to take him to a doctor, who told them both that Bert was suffering from nervous ailments which would probably pass after he got married.

While they were listening to the doctor, Doris was squeezing Bert's sweating hand under the desk. The shame that he always felt when he shook hands, because of his wet palms, was curiously absent with Doris. Gradually his sense of gratitude had developed into a need for her that could only be likened to what he felt for mama. Soon she was coming into his room when his lights were out, sitting on his bed, smoothing his cheek and stroking his hair. She became his solace and his refuge. Doris must have known that here was a chance for her to get a position she had always envied— the security she could achieve because of Bert's need of her.

One evening when Harold and Mother went to the theater, and Doris was certain they would not return for hours, she got into bed with Bert. "I didn't quite know what was happening to me," he said. "She was doing things I never dreamed of before. We had sexual intercourse. When it was over, I asked her to marry me. She said she loved me and she knew that marrying me was what mama would have wanted."

Mother didn't object to the marriage. In fact, she gave Bert her diamond ring to give to Doris, and took a large part in all their arrangements. After the marriage, however, when Mother suggested they all live together, Doris objected, and the newlyweds took an apartment by themselves.

Bert was a devoted husband. He placed his wife on a pedestal, as he had his mother and brother. Their wishes were his commands. Mother thought the boys should go into business for themselves. By this time Harold had married, too, but was not doing well in his job. Doris knew that Bert was much more industrious and more of a go-getter than his brother, who was dependent on him more and more, but she assented to the partnership plan. Without her consent Bert would not have gone ahead.

Although Bert continued his hypochondriacal complaints, and vistited doctors frequently, his efforts and industry soon brought the partners great success in their sporting goods equipment stores. As the business developed and became increasingly demanding and time-consuming, Bert had less time for doctors. Indeed, he had less time for anything but his business, which he built into a big corporation.

Doris wanted a large family and had four children in rapid succession. She claimed to adore them, but actually she had no mothering instincts and left them to the care of nurses or maids, who were frequently changed. Doris spent her time in the shops and at the beauty parlor. She had little interest in caring for the house, simply scribbling instructions about what should be ordered at the grocer's and tossing them to one of the maids, who would phone the store.

When Bert was thirty-seven, Mother died. Bert had not only provided for her luxuriously from the business, but he was supplying his brother and his wife and their two children in the same fashion. He had built a beautiful home for Doris and his own children and gave them everything they could possibly wish for. Doris had lovely clothes, servants, all the luxuries obtainable—and all the authority previously held by Mother.

But a discrepancy had been developing slowly in Bert's life through the years. He was the mastermind of a huge business, treated with awe and respect by people of whom he himself was awe-stricken and frightened—bankers, manufacturers, even his competitors. Yet at home he was the last to be considered, the most ignored, the most insignificant. When he came into the house, nobody emerged to greet him. At the table he sat in no position of distinction, but when Harold visited, the high-backed chair was placed at the head of the table and Harold sat there with pompous pride. What Bert cared to eat was completely ignored. Whatever he especially liked was invariably spoiled in the cooking. Even the servants, in some subtle way, had been conditioned to ignore and disrespect his needs. Doris was the undisputed queen in his house.

Bert was not consciously aware of this diminution in his constellation. He held his position of insignificance as a matter of fact and made everyone around him more important. When any privileges or priorities were at issue, such as who would be served first, or who would be deferred to in opinions, Bert immediately assumed an inferior position, pushing his wife or his brother, whom he worshipped and grossly overestimated, into the spotlight.

Doris and Harold devoured all this with as little questioning or guilt as there was obligation or tendency to give back. Bert invited no special regard, and by his masochistic needs he tempted Doris toward the sadistic role Mother had previously enjoyed by giving it to her as a gift. Naturally Doris seized it. But where Mother had been a seasoned matriarch Doris was an upstart. She used her power unrestrainedly and recklessly. She was so drunk with it that she could not even be concerned that her own children were swept aside in the wake of it.

Bert's devotion to the members of his family could be described only as lavish. He had the same feeling of worship for them that he had felt for Mother and Harold in his early years. His family always came first. There was, however, a rigidity in it. Those who were the recipients of his love and generosity took from him, but also recoiled from him defensively. They must have sensed that beneath the façade of generosity there was hate. Indeed, the hatred was as constant as the stream of life itself that yearned for the love his hatred would compel.

Such forces, when they are in operation, do not stand still. Gravity may pull with varying strengths through different media. An object falls more quickly in atmosphere than it does in water. Standing on one kind of earth gives more support against its pull than another. Bert was standing in quicksand, and the rate of his unconscious tendencies toward regression was accelerated.

The breaking point came when Harold was injured in an automobile accident while Bert was driving. Harold's foot was mangled. In a frenzy, Bert took off his brother's shoe and saw the blood pouring out. Looking up then into Harold's face, he saw there an expression of complete calm that spelled out to him as clearly as though his brother had spoken: *Nothing can happen to me.*

At that moment, Bert experienced panic. If nothing could happen to Harold, it meant, on the archaic level of their relationship, that everything could happen to him. A volcanic surge of remembered vilifications, condemnations and threats he had endured at the hands of his sadistic mother during early childhood washed over him. He had a feeling that he himself would be mutilated and mangled momentarily. Harold was the injured one, but Bert had to be treated for shock, and even then his panic abated only slightly.

This traumatic experience was followed by other shocking events. Harold became reckless with money, and with ill-conceived plans for the organization. Doris was constantly more extravagant and added abuse to disregard when her husband admonished her. Bert's children sullenly ignored him even more. He began to bargain desperately to avert the increasingly threatening collapse in the economy of his business and his home. In his panic, he was driven to pay an even greater price to win his wife's love and his brother's regard. But the more he bargained and gave, the less he got, and the less he got, the more he paid. At last he reached a position where the anxiety that gave way intermittently to panic was constantly upon him.

The Matriarch

Now the only way he could get any attention was to be sick. Harold, however, was basically as indifferent as one sperm is to another. As for Doris, she had an old score to settle—her mother's abandonment of her when she was a child, to take care of Bert. She had to be the one who did the abandoning now, and this was just the critical situation she needed to rid herself finally of being the abandoned one in the symbols of her childhood.

When sickness failed to get Bert the attention he needed from Doris and Harold, the hatred he harbored against them was turned back on himself and he began to stew, so to speak, in his own juices. He lost all hope. A feeling of futility and impending annihilation overtook him. This kind of helplessness would have led him ultimately to suicide as the final instrumentalization that would return him to Mother, whose love was his eternal quest.

Bert's reaction in his first session indicated his potential for recovering the will to live. When he gave me the opportunity to knock brains into his head, or to knock his brains out, thereby offering me the role of him who gives or takes away—that is, deification, I declined, and waited for a more realistic and personal offering.

I knew that if we could establish a relationship in which both of us were human beings, with no proposition of dehumanization, our association would progress and my patient could begin his journey back to his beginnings and rise again on his own power, rather than the power of a usurper who humiliated, degraded and desexualized him psychically so that he had no anti-gravity capacity of his own.

When, in that first session, he asked me whether I used shock treatment, and I told him about my procedure, he was surprised to find a person who would not be tempted by his masochistic invitation. I realized then that he was capable of another kind of relationship. Before he left the session, he told me he didn't understand it, but he felt hopeful for the first time in years.

Chapter 5

The Patriarch

The patriarch is the male head of a graded system—a family, a community or a state. In this graded system, he may also be the head of a business, school, system of beliefs, religious order, or cause. "Graded" means a system ranging from high grade to low grade, with the implication that the patriarch is the "high" and everyone else is the "low." Men may be created equal, but in their relationships to others they immediately become unequal and remain so. This is often a tragic circumstance.

To most of us a patriarch is a venerable old man, but that is really a misconception. In contradistinction to the man, the patriarch is not the head for the good of all but rather for his own good. In his mind, being at the head makes him better, stronger, faster and higher than all others. He professes loudly that he is in his position for the good of all, but it is actually incidental to his primary aspirations, not his chief concern.

He does not care whether anything or anybody else is secondary, but he will battle to the death anyone who tries to usurp his position as head.

Now we see that he is not unlike the preconceptual sperm. If he had been vital enough to combine, to become mutual and coalesce with an ovum, he would have become the man, and as such he would be the humane head of a group of human beings whom he would have no need to degrade within the system.

The patriarch is a psychically desexualized man. He is a poor lover, a bad husband and a worse father. For all the material benefits he gives his family, there is no spiritual quality in his relationship with them. He may take away the benefits at any time. He rules with an iron fist, and with infantile (pregenital) power devices, and he is capable of devastating wrath. The patriarch never appears in the psychoanalyst's office for help, but his wife and children do.

One of my colleagues called one day to ask if I would see a patient for supportive therapy. Consenting, I expected to see an individual from whom little could be hoped for as far as achieving a cure was concerned. The technical term "supportive therapy" implies that a patient will not be able to live satisfactorily under his own power but will have to be helped permanently.

The patient's name was Joanne. She was twenty-six years old at the time, a plump, rather girlish kind of woman, well built and with good features. Her hair was pushed casually over on one side and hung to her shoulders in careless fashion, but otherwise she was fairly well groomed. In her expression there was an "unfinished" quality, an indirection, as though she were waiting for some kind of settlement. Glancing at me occasionally, her eyes appealed and questioned, saying, "Will you please understand me, and not beat me down?"

In our first session, much to my surprise, I detected the kind of warmth not usually found in a patient with this kind of introduction. Though she carried with her the stigma of having been shifted from one analyst to another, to which she was not insensitive, I thought she bore it with a dignity which could only have been the result of her own astuteness.

The doctor is trained to look for symptoms of sickness, but very often he can discern some areas of brightness among the shadows if he looks for symptoms of health.

Although she was despairing and discouraged, and dissociated from reality to some extent, Joanne caused me to have enough feeling for her so that a rapport was established between us which led me to think we could make the climb.

She talked of her divorce. At first the reasons for it were obscure, as she explained them. Her husband's family was rich. Her husband was a nice boy, though very spoiled. They had to live in Milwaukee, where his family had a business, but there were so many of them, uncles and aunts and cousins, and their ways were so different from hers that she became more confused every day. By the time her second child was born everything was becoming too much for her, and she knew she had to get away, to be free of her husband and his family. That was why she came back to New York to be with her own family and divorced him. No, she said, she didn't live with her parents. She had her own apartment and was taking care of her two children.

As I listened to her and observed, she appeared like a child rambling on, easily and trustingly, as though the listener were native and friendly. A woman so childish and trusting can be said to visualize a horizon and a future, needing only someone good enough and kind enough to help her.

Later in our work, when the fog in her mind lifted, Joanne was able to organize her thinking and give me more details about her marriage. Her husband, Ralph, was the first-born of socially prominent parents. Social position is usually thought of as glamorous, but in reality it often takes a great toll and prevents a woman from performing the more natural functions of motherhood. Ralph's mother was so circumscribed, and he suffered from this lack in her.

Similarly, wealthy boys often fail to benefit from the material advantages which are theirs. They are usually brought up by nurses, governesses and tutors. As one becomes more educated to what takes place realistically between human beings who are thrown together exclusively and secretly, it is clear that exceptional care must be taken in exposing a helpless infant or child to caretakers. Enough has not been said and written about what a nursemaid or a governess can do to the one with whom she is entrusted.

Ralph not only hated his legitimate mother, and tried by his infantile power device to force her back to him, but he also hated his "illegitimate" mothers, a series of nursemaids who too often ignored, neglected and punished him. When his hatred of them also failed, he fell back to a previous phase of disorganization, namely, rage reactions. Though Ralph, as an adult, had all the manners and social graces and the physical appearance of good grooming, Joanne discovered shortly after she started to live with him that he was a disturbed, irritable and destructive infant. Joanne was incapable of mature affection and sexual love, but Ralph was even less capable. His ideas were not much more advanced than those of the tomcat who beats his female into submission, having no tendency to woo, entice or persuade, as do others in the animal kingdom. Not only was he primitive in his sexual aggression towards her, but the episodes were of such short duration that they were virtually over before they started. Probably this was because he thought subconsciously to escape before he had to endure the retaliation he anticipated from his wife. In other words, he ejaculated to get the thing over with quickly, for fear of what might happen to him when his penis got into that dark enclosure.

Naturally, Joanne's life was empty and the richness around her, as far as her own living economy was concerned, was fraudulent. When her parents visited her after the birth of her second child, they found her unwilling to get out of bed. She had an obvious lack of interest not only in her newborn child but in them, or in anything else. Her father assessed the situation and made a quick decision. She was to come back to New York immediately and get a divorce. Joanne offered no resistance.

When she was settled again in New York, her family doctor found her to be disturbed and depressed, living excessively in isolation and fantasy, and he recommended she be put under psychiatric care. When her condition failed to improve, her psychiatrist referred her to me for supportive treatment.

One day, during a session, I put a significant question to her: "What about your own family, Joanne. Tell me about them." Instantly her features grew tense. She was startled out of the peaceful fantasy she had been enjoying. Speaking noticeably faster, she told me: "My father always gave me everything. He says I don't need an analyst at all. He said my brother's analysis was a waste of money, and my sister's, too. He gives me everything I need. He said I should just go ahead and find myself another husband. My mother thinks I had no right to get divorced, that I should have thought of my children and my parents before I took such a step."

The story began to emerge. Joanne was the second-born. Her sister was four years older, and her brother six years younger. Both were still unmarried. Her father was the fifth son of a large family of underprivileged and underdeveloped people, a great many of whom were dependent on his benevolence to get along. He was wooed, flattered and made into a god by his brothers and sisters, a position he enjoyed completely. But because they made him feel like a god they expected the benevolences of one from him.

This state of affairs was inimical to his wife's self-interest. Joanne's mother also came from a deprived home. Her father had been a music teacher in love with his art to the point where it made little difference to him whether his pupils paid him or not. This lack of realism, however, compelled his wife to take in roomers to eke out a living. Joanne's mother, Lily, was a handsome, ambitious woman, determined not to be dependent on a man for her security. Lily was convinced that men were inferior because her mother was the main support and the most reliable wage earner in her family.

When she met Sam Gilbert, Joanne's father, she found him interesting not only because he could take her out of the poverty in which she lived, but because through him she could show her father what he should have been, and show her mother the kind of husband she should have gotten in order to give her the happy childhood she had never had. Lily's marriage was a triumph. It was a reproof to her parents for not providing her with the good things of life. She was able to queen it over them, and over her sisters and brothers, because she had acquired these material benefits for herself by making a successful marriage.

Obviously Joanne's mother was still seeking for that happy childhood of which she had been deprived. A person who yearns constantly for this fantasied time of happiness competes with all others, including her own husband and children, to acquire it. Mrs. Gilbert resented unconsciously the important position her husband held in his own family. Because of her aspirations, she had to whittle him down, keep him in hand, so to speak. Although she seemed to be an ideal wife, actually her favors were devisive in a hundred subtle ways. Her ultimate goals had more to do with these aspirations than her husband's welfare.

Her unconscious technique was to treat him like a little boy, to be the good mother she shrewdly suspected he had always wanted and never had. She made herself indispensable to him, but in a way that broke him down and was designed to make him incapable of doing things for himself. This pernicious relationship, intended to undermine him, rendered this "great god" incapable of picking out his own necktie. She talked him into believing he was color blind. He could not pack a bag for himself when he went on a trip because he always forgot the essentials, and he could not buy a suitable gift for anyone because he did not have his wife's exquisite taste. The effect of this "spoiling," all of it accomplished in the name of love, was to flatter him and inflate his infantilized ego even more than the adulation of his grasping relatives.

Sam Gilbert was bitterly disappointed when his first child was a girl. In fact, he didn't want to take a chance on a second. When Joanne was born, he was seriously depressed, but he overcame his frustration by proving himself superior in other ways. He became a power in various business enterprises and on committees involved in good works, in order to re-establish his self-esteem. Unable to wield power over him to the extent she had before, Mrs. Gilbert founded a school for underprivileged children, which she could head and thus become the supreme power in her own right.

Now Joanne was exposed to nurses, and to her resentful, hostile older sister, Anne, whose treatment of her was sadistic and depriving. When Joanne was three years old, it had dawned on her parents through the remarks of others that she was an exceptionally beautiful child. By this time they had experienced feelings of distance from her, which Anne thought she had created. Anne believed she had been successful in keeping her father and mother away from her younger sister, but Joanne thought it was her own fault they kept away from her.

Later, as the parents began to draw near, each said in effect to the other: Keep away from her; she's mine. Thus Joanne became the competitive prize for each parent, a prize neither could win because each pushed the other aside, leaving Joanne still the alone and lonely one. When the parents did have the chance to be alone with her, they lavished so much emotion and excitement on the child, because of the guilt they experienced, that Joanne became overstimulated. In order to relieve these tensions, she engaged compulsively in auto-erotic activity. This terrified the parents because she made no attempt to conceal it, in spite of threats and intimidation. It was her special way of gaining control and holding the attention of her parents. Now she was able to bring them to her.

The doctors who were called in to deal with this condition could achieve no success with their remedies, of course, because nothing short of analysis would have relieved such compulsive masturbation. Joanne had no intention of relinquishing her power device. The struggle with her parents to control it, however, became so keen that masturbation was an obsession and a constant preoccupation, even after six years of age, when such activity normally ceases. Joanne was still the peculiar one, the shunned, shamed and guilty one.

As though she had not enough trauma in her life, her mother gave birth to a son when Joanne was six, and the boy became the apple of his parents' eye. In order to be noticed at all, and to bring the attention that would make them aware of her, Joanne continued to be a "problem" child. She had to be incorrect, wrong and recalcitrant. She felt that it was the only way she would be noticed, tended and cared for. There were no parents in this family. They were all children, all in perpetual rivalry with each other.

During this time another turn was taking place in the affairs of the family. Joanne's father was increasingly successful in business and adapted easily to the manners and patterns of the very rich man. He acquired all the outward show of wealth and success. He joined clubs, served on philanthropic committees, acquired the speech, manners and attitudes of a man of wealth. Propriety and decorum were the outward standards, but at bottom money remained his god.

His wife gave up her school and devoted herself more and more to her husband. Now that he had achieved nation-wide fame, she could gain more prestige for herself by basking in the sunshine of his glory than she could in her personal undertakings. However, though she gained more prestige, she suffered a loss of security and as a result became somewhat of a clinging vine, so that her children were deprived even more of attention and devotion while her husband gained the satisfaction of the exclusiveness of the mother-child relationship he had always yearned for.

Indeed, if she diverted any attention from him to the children, he resented it and punished her as well as the children by sullen silences and disapproval. His wife and children had to subordinate themselves to him, to think and behave in a way that complimented his position.

Joanne, however, continued to be "different." She rebelled against the existing pattern, defiant of the rigidities and regulations laid down by her father. By the time she got to high school, she began to think for herself, although her thinking was not as organized and developed as it might have been. Her marriage to Ralph was a flight from her home. One of the inducements was that she would be living halfway across the country from her father. What she hadn't reckoned with, however, was that she might be jumping from the frying pan into the fire.

I discovered in my sessions with Joanne that potentially she was more capable of health than all the other members of the family.

After several months of analysis, Joanne began to bloom. Where her coloring and her attitudes had been dimmed by years of unrelatedness, now she became radiant and animated because of being recognized and appreciated and getting to understand herself. Once again she regained her original beauty.

At this point an unusual event took place. Her father called and declared that he and his wife wanted to meet me. The session was pleasant. It was cheering to me to hear parents so grateful and so warm in their praise. There was much joviality and hearty hand-shaking when they left my office. Next morning, however, Mr. Gilbert called me again. He told me he was worried. Shouldn't we have a consultation with another analyst about his daughter's mental health? He hadn't slept all night. He wanted to make sure his daughter was in the right hands, that she was getting everything that could possibly be obtained to restore her health.

It was, of course, a most unusual request to make in a psycho-analytic situation, particularly when the results were so good. I told him this, and reminded him of his elation the day before, but he argued energetically that this was not an uncommon procedure among doctors, and he could very well afford such a consultation. He was most persistent, so I told him I would discuss the matter with Joanne and let him know.

That day, when Joanne came for her session, I told her what had occurred. A twisted smile appeared on her lips, and I could almost read her mind. I knew she was thinking about her father, saying to herself, *He can't stand it.*

After a moment she asked in a strained voice, "What are you going to do?"

"This is your analysis, Joanne," I answered. "What do you want me to do?"

She told me then that her father had to have his way, and if I refused, he would take it out not only on her, but on her sister and brother and mother. Her father simply would brook no interference in any plan of his own making. This comment was further evidence that Joanne not only was healthier than the others in her family who were knuckling under to the father, but now she was able to maintain her healthiness in the face of the father's threatened aggression. Therefore I assented to his demand.

When his selected analyst reported to him that everything was in order and he could find no fault with Joanne's analysis, Mr. Gilbert's fear that things might not go right with his daughter (the conscious fear is the unconscious wish) quieted down, temporarily at least, and the analysis proceeded.

As Joanne became more and more capable of standing on her own feet and making a go of things, many more such consultations with psychiatrists were demanded. It might surprise many of my colleagues, yet the method of procedure I had to take to save Joanne's mind was of such a nature as to make Mr. Gilbert's demands understandable. Though I battled him all the way, I was sympathetic with him behind my overt attitudes. He had to be first and foremost. Not only did he compete with his wife and children, but he had to compete with me. My creativeness with his daughter put him in the unbearable position of being secondary. In his mind, and in his emotional reactions, that could be equated with losing his grip on life.

I anticipated his reactions to Joanne's improvement, and I warned her that every advance she made into the field of reality activity and independence would be a threat to her father and that she would experience more and more pressure from him.

One day when she stood up to him, he shouted at her furiously that she was crazy. Following that scene, she came to her session depressed and discouraged, and I decided to call for another meeting of Joanne, her parents and myself.

At this session, I attempted to point out to the parents that although Joanne had been extremely sick before, she had made great progress in her strivings toward mental health, and I enumerated her gains. But before I could finish, her father jumped up excitedly and began to pace the floor and talk about his own struggles, what he had accomplished against what odds; how his success was greater than anybody's he had ever known.

When he finished, I turned to Joanne and said quietly but firmly, "Joanne, what you just witnessed is the kind of thing you are going to face all your life, consciously or unconsciously. Your father—and you just heard him—is competing with you as though you were the same age and the same size, and out for the same goal. Your mother hasn't said anything, but I think you should know that she is as much a child as your father. You will have to learn to be your own parent and stop looking for one. I also want you to know that I consider your parents as innocent of what they are doing as I consider you innocent. Their parents did no better for them. This immaturity is all of our inheritance."

At this point Mr. Gilbert jumped to his feet, grabbed his coat angrily, and, commanding his wife to come along with him, stalked out of my office, slamming the door. He was not beaten, however. All told, seven consultations took place before he found an analyst who agreed with him that Joanne should finish her analysis with someone else.

But Joanne refused to do it. By this time she had achieved enough understanding of what her problem was so that she needed no further analysis. She knew that her father, because he controlled the money, also felt he controlled the destinies of his own family, and of his brothers and sisters and their families who were dependent on him. In his own mind he was a superman—in short, a patriarch.

What he could not know, and what no one could tell him, was that he was a psychically desexualized man, and as such he did not possess his highest faculties that would enable him to maintain a grip on his current reality, remain with it and adapt to it. In spite of his power front, Mr. Gilbert knew himself unconsciously as an individual who might, at any time, lose the goal of his aspirations, namely, a span of life as the first and foremost.

To the psychically desexualized man, everybody is his competitor. Anybody who achieves a goal successfully that in any way affects him is envied. It produces jealousy in him and mobilizes his senseless aggression to tear them down. In his neurotic thinking, I became the aggressive competitor who was undermining his power over his daughter, so he had to get rid of me as the first step in his unconscious campaign to keep Joanne dependent on him by forcing her back into a state of mental and emotional instability.

Mr. Gilbert could control, dominate and keep in line the "sick" Joanne, in whose symbol systems he could rid himself of his unwanted feelings of weakness and inferiority. She was dependent on him for money, and as a mentally and emotionally disturbed person she was forced to obey him, listen to him, and look to him for advice, aid and succor. He was in the driver's seat, controlling her destiny as long as she remained sick.

Joanne had always been different, rebellious and a problem. As a well person, she resented and questioned his commands and his orders. Her ideas conflicted with his, and she became the only one he could not dominate and bully. My success with her belittled him and made him seem insignificant to himself, prompting him, instinctively, to act like a weak sperm and make all the other sperm weaker than himself. By impugning me, he had hoped he might interfere and weaken the analytic process that was making his daughter healthy.

When his efforts failed, Mr. Gilbert cut Joanne's allowance, as a final desperate gesture to make his power felt. With only her alimony, Joanne and her two children had to live on a scale far below that of her parents and her sister and brother, but she was able to do so—even took pride in being able to get along without her father's help. In fact, the experience proved to her that she did not have to be sick so that her father could prove himself to be the good provider for the sick and helpless.

An important factor that helped Joanne achieve full mental growth was that her analyst did not find himself blocked by any taboo or prohibition from examining the nature of her father and mother. Identifying with her analyst, Joanne became unafraid to look and judge. She came to understand that she had been exploited since her earliest childhood. Though she had been born to a life of material plenty, there was, unfortunately, an emotional scarcity in the soil in which she grew up. She came to know that she could not look to her father, mother, sister or brother for help. She would have to develop her own motor power and her own consciousness to be able to deal with the novel situations arising in the living reality about her.

Joanne came to see that hating her parents was nothing more than an infantile device to force them to give her parental love, of which they were incapable because they had never received it, and had never known it themselves.

There was one goal I had with Joanne that I did not achieve—to bring her closer to her family. She was willing, but when she approached them with positive attitudes, and attempted at the same time to maintain her dignity and self-respect, there would be an ever-present content in the attitudes of both her parents to belittle, degrade and humiliate her with grandiose gestures and condescending attitudes. It was impossible to be close with them, and Joanne had to learn to make her symbol systems impervious to their thrusts.

Through analysis, Joanne learned that she did not have to yearn for better ancestors, but that she herself could be the better ancestor to her own two children and their descendants.

Chapter 6

The Jungle Within

In their early days, children have their souls in their eyes, and what is on their minds is also on their tongues for mama to hear. But as they grow a little older, and have the shocking experiences described in the early chapters of this book, they soon learn to hide what they feel and what they are. They develop a façade, the meaning of which is disappointing to those who like to think "God's in His heaven, all's right with the world." The façade implies that the child has put his best foot forward; it often conceals inferiority and malevolence stalking behind it.

The word "personality" is derived from the Latin "persona," which originally meant a face mask, used by actors to portray a character. Our own personalities are a synthesis comprised of acquired layers of identification, socializations and acculturations. On the floor of the personality structure lives the original savage, the megalomaniac and the infant who is omnipotent. If the personality is deep and well put together—in short, a good insulator—it will contain successfully the volcanic eruptions that spring up from this floor.

A man's malevolence may be contained within himself or within his family, but if a man's egomania is strong enough he may be able to break out into the community and from there into the outside world, spreading his baleful influence wherever he appears. If the family is strong enough, it will be able to drive these unsocial and savage forces back into the man to endure within himself, but if these forces succeed in breaking through the individual's insulation, overpowering the family and appearing in the outside world, the area they can encompass is limited only by the insulation the outside world is able to build up against him.

The Jungle Within

All this is illustrated by the story of Barbara. When she appeared in my office for the first time, she carried a package under her arm. As the session went on, she unwrapped it and produced a manuscript about a girl named Babette, who was supposedly a fictional character but undoubtedly referred to herself.

Barbara was about four feet, ten inches tall and built attractively in proportion. In the fashion of the day, the coat she wore had shoulders padded to an extreme so that she looked almost as broad as she was tall. She was thirty-eight years old, but she had the face of a blonde doll, with large, round blue eyes like a baby's.

Her speech was elemental as she described her unhappiness. She came to me, she said, not because she needed any help for herself, but because her sister-in-law, who had been analyzed by me several years before, had suggested to her that if she knew more about people it would be better for her sons and her husband. Recalling what the sister-in-law had told me during the analysis, I knew what a hellcat Barbara was, and I wondered how a woman so angelic in appearance could be capable of such an act as banging her son's head against the faucet in the bathtub, injuring him so severely he had to be taken to a hospital. I knew, too, that she was given to throwing things at whoever happened to be the victim of her wrath momentarily.

The story she had written and left with me was conceived with the mentality one would expect from a six-year-old. It was the wish fulfillment in fantasy of all she lacked in reality, what is known clinically as "family-romance" and in literature as the Cinderella story. Usually these stories are created by those who have to comfort themselves by wish-fulfilling dreams and fantasies because of a paucity of love and affection and good things in their early days. They imagine themselves to be children of kings, nobility, millionaires and other important figures. In more severe disturbances, they pose as such figures and come to believe they are descended from them.

Barbara told me she did not feel sick, but she was dissatisfied because her husband paid very little attention to her. He came home late at night, hardly ever spoke to her, and refused to have sexual intercourse. But for herself, she insisted, there was nothing wrong with her mind. She had no anxiety, no depression, no guilt feelings, and no physical sickness. But in view of the aggressions I knew about, and the fact that her husband would have no sexual relationship with her, I diagnosed her in my mind as a severe character disorder.

People who suffer from character disorder are not aware they have any mental defects. They have relieved themselves of shame, anxiety and guilt by developing character traits that banish such feelings, as superstitious people banish anxiety by a ritual, a magic gesture or a word. They can be so aggressive that their disturbances no longer exist in their own symbol systems, having been disposed of into the symbols of others in their constellation who are suffering for them. Such people refuse to go to an analyst, and one can hardly blame them, for that would mean that their character defenses would be broken down and they would begin to suffer from the feelings they had successfully projected onto others.

Living beings do not want pain. Even the masochist enjoys it only because the pain he is experiencing is less than he anticipates he might be experiencing. In other words, he makes bargains in a fantastic manner, paying off, so to speak, with less suffering than he expected to have.

In this respect, Barbara posed a very difficult problem. How could I have her continue to visit me when our association must necessarily cause her more and more pain, for which the gains would be beyond her ability to realize? Further, the reality she was creating in her life was bound to boomerang; in fact, it had caught up with her already. She had lost her husband's love and association, a loss for which she was not taking the blame. She had projected it, accusing him of having these dispositions toward her through no fault of her own. He was the bad one, the disloyal and cruel one.

Her home was scarcely a peaceful haven. Her oldest son, Jack, who was thirteen years old at the time, constantly bought guns which were displayed all over his room. He kept one under his pillow at night. Her second son, Eddie, two years younger than Jack, also outfitted himself with weapons, but his interest was more in switchblade knives, brass knuckles, blackjacks and similar devices. The third son, Ralph, whom she called her doll, had no such interests. He was the one she really loved and who loved her. I learned later that he was distinctly feminine in his way of talking and walking and in his interests.

Bickering, wrangling and violence were constant in this house. Ralph, constantly teased, was nearly always crying. Eddie used foul language exclusively. Jack often threatened to crack his mother's head or throw her out the window. Barbara's husband, as she described him, walked about the house like one apart, quiet and vague, coming and going without noticing or being noticed. Needless to say, this was a devastated home.

Barbara was frequently called to school and argued with her husband which of them should go. There were no complaints about Ralph, who was his teacher's pet, but Jack and Eddie were the troublemakers in their classes. Theirs was the kind of insolence that knows no bounds. Apparently they were as likely to tell the teacher or the principal to "drop dead" as to wish him good morning. As Barbara described this situation, there was no evidence that she had any idea of her own responsibility in the development of her three sons, or their effect on her husband's disposition. If, during our first year of work, I had given her any idea that she was responsible, I would never have seen her again.

The task of the analyst is often one that would baffle the imagination if the analyst had not been analyzed himself. What I had to do in this situation was to remember what a young man does when he falls in love. He overevaluates the good and underestimates the bad. He represses his negative feelings, thereby experiencing a pure strain of the positive. If I had been moralistic in my consideration of Barbara, or if I had had a need to rid myself of self-contempt, I would have judged her and she would have felt it.

Therefore I overevaluated Barbara, kept her virtues in the foreground, and ignored her flaws. But at the same time I maintained a realistic vigil over those faults which would have to be dealt with at a more propitious time. To have permitted them to remain uncorrected would have amounted to the perpetuation of the tragic family which Barbara had created.

The psychoanalyst is specialized in treating his patient primarily for the patient's sake, but in accordance with the conceptions postulated in this book his patient is not only an individual but also part of a family. Barbara had created the kind of family she lived with because she had to externalize the family that had been internalized in her early childhood.

Barbara was four years old when her mother died. Her maternal relatives were particularly clannish, primitive people. Her father was considered of inferior caste and was rudely ejected from the family. She and her brother were taken to be reared by two aunts who lived in different houses. Her brother died of rheumatic heart disease when he was twenty-four years old; it was the same ailment that had killed her mother. Barbara was never permitted to see her father.

The aunt to whom she had the bad fortune to be given was an austere, severe and dominating mother of three sons and two daughters, the overpowering wife of a timid husband who was steeped in religion. Although they had immigrated to this country more than two decades previously, they had departed very little from their former culture.

Visiting relatives gave a great deal of righteous attention to Barbara, as did her aunt and uncle. She was always questioned about her shoes and stockings. Did she have enough dresses? Did she like the food? Did she get as much as the other children? She had become a cause, and the burden of it overwhelmed her. Barbara was like a lost waif for whom innumerable hands were clutching to perform their charitable deeds, so that they might demonstrate to each other how big-hearted they were.

When she was alone with any of these "benevolent" people, however, she could sense the chill of the emptiness of their interest in her. When the uncle with whom she lived came home with dolls for his two girls, there would be none for her. The dresses bought for her were like the ones her cousins wore for visiting days but of a different kind for other days. At table, she was quite naturally served last, but not infrequently got the food of the day before while her cousins were given the fresh food. All this, of course, she never dared to mention, but on occasion she burst forth with some kind of behavior not at all understandable to her benefactors. For example, there were areas of her head where she had pulled out her hair, and on two occasions she had tried to rip her mouth apart with her two index fingers.

The aunt, who was very pious, questioned her daily about whether any of her sons had molested her, and she watched the boys closely. Barbara was warned constantly that if she gave any boy a chance he would "ruin" her, ruin being thus equated with any sexual activity.

When she was eight, Barbara discovered that she was far more agile than most of the other girls. She became athletic and took part in all the rowdy activities the boys on her block would permit her to join. They liked her tininess, prettiness and spunk, and she was soon their mascot and pet. As time went on, Barbara insisted, she even became their leader because she was able to do better than they did in all their sports.

The most striking recollection she could produce from the time span covered by her residence with her aunt until she married was the sadism of this woman, whom she always referred to as "the old witch." The beatings she took were not on the buttocks, as with the other children, but on her head and with unmitigated violence. Of course this never took place when any of the relatives were around —in fact, it almost never took place when any of the other children were around. Barbara knew when to expect her aunt's wrath, and she conditioned herself to go through it and get it over with. Later, on deeper analysis, I learned that her aunt was not the only one who instigated these activities, and that Barbara could have escaped them and did not. Indeed, she frequently invited them.

There was a peculiar value placed in this home on certain kinds of violence. For example, the first time she began to menstruate, Barbara recalled, her aunt assumed a terrified expression and "slapped my face so hard, I thought she'd knocked my teeth out."

It should be explained that the slap itself is the motor expression, operating through the muscular system, of an impulse originating in the deepest symbols of the unconscious. It amounts to panto-miming, through the motor apparatus, the primeval idea: "You are what you are, because I make you," or, "It is so because I make it so." A slap is the method used by the primitive mother in awakening her daughter symbolically to sexuality. The fairy tale of Snow White expresses this idea when the bewitched little girl is awakened with a kiss. The discharge of violence is gratifying to the one who does the slapping. It is a substitute for sexual satisfaction on the sadistic level and is basically a homosexual activity.

Barbara suffered a similar slapping at the hands of her cousin, who was about six years older, when he saw her put on lipstick for the first time. In both instances, Barbara said, the faces of those who did the slapping were transported, as though they were saving her soul.

Until she was nineteen, Barbara was not permitted to be out after dark, and when she did have a boy visiting her they were never allowed to be in a room alone together. She was still meticulously examined by all the relatives concerned with her welfare, and she had to fulfill all the requirements of propriety, which, for the most part, were concerned with her desexualization. Her aunt not only admonished her daily but also suspected her of activities in which she could not possibly have been involved. The aunt had been growing progressively stranger, and her actions were increasingly less rational. Sometimes she got up in the night and put on her wedding gown and walked around the house with her elbow bent as though someone were leading her to the altar. She could be heard holding extensive conversations in her room with imaginary people. Her husband, who was frail and meek, feared her as he would the devil.

The relatives got together and decided to send Barbara to a business school to learn stenography and typing. Afterward, she was placed in the firm of a relative where she could be watched. There she met her husband, whose family was known and approved by her family. She was very pretty in those days. Louis was nice to her, and they were married. "When Lou proposed to me," Barbara said, "I was very happy. He had a wonderful family."

The Jungle Within

Barbara described the early days of her marriage as life in a love nest. When her husband came home at night, a table was set for him that would have pleased a gourmet. She stood at the window and watched for him, so that he could wave to her and she could wave back as he approached the house. As he walked to the bus in the morning, she stood again at the window and kept her eyes on him until he turned the corner, waving to her for the last time as he did so.

Curiously, Barbara's recitals of her marriage idyll did not ring true. It sounded like a fairy tale, or a dream she was making up. Undoubtedly these activities had occurred, more or less as she recalled them, but they had no more meaning than a ritual. Her husband, as I came to know later, always experienced a strong feeling of deprivation when he participated in these same activities. Although his wife went through the physical motions, he sensed the emptiness of these devotions.

He said he felt as though they were unreal, that they were both play-acting. And Barbara *was* play-acting. The child who had moved into the desert that was her aunt's house had then and there become fixated at the four-year-old level of emotional development.

At the time Louis' sister sent Barbara to me, his brother sent Louis to another analyst. After a year and a half of his analysis, Louis insisted on coming to see me. He wanted to know if I would be willing to treat him concurrently with his wife. I reserved decision about accepting him as a patient until I talked to Barbara. For reasons that will be clear later, I told her I was disinclined to treat her husband. Barbara, however, was insistent that I do so, and I finally agreed, not only because she wanted me to treat her husband but because the two older boys, as well as Lou, were getting progressively out of hand, to the point where some kind of disaster could have occurred at any time. These people not only needed an analyst, they needed an active arbitrator and conciliator.

As Barbara had become increasingly well enough supplied in her analytical relationship with me, and gained confidence and self-esteem, Lou had progressively lost these attributes. At the same time, according to his analyst and my observation, he had become extremely sick. He was diffuse, vague and depressed. In addition, his attitudes and activities in his place of business were bizarre. He absented himself at the most significant times and failed to appear at the most important appointments. He had picked up a compliant woman or two and spent sums of money on them that he could ill afford. He did not keep his extra-marital affairs secret, but talked about them defiantly even to his wife, as though he were saying: "Well, what are you going to do about it?"

When he reported these activities to me, looking for criticism or approval or direction, I merely manifested an interest in why he was doing these things, and when he pressed me for an opinion I said, "These activities must have their meaning, and in due time we'll find out what it is." I had concluded that his behavior represented a gradual decompression, which had been saving him from some kind of explosion.

After I had worked with them concurrently for a year, it became evident that what Louis wanted was to separate me from his wife so that he could be in analysis with me alone.

Lou's rationalization was a clever one. He knew that his wife's chief complaint was that he refused to have sexual intercourse with her, and he knew, too, that if he did have intercourse with her it would prove to me that my work with them was successful. Therefore he offered the argument that he could not have intercourse with his wife because he would have to talk about it to me; she would also tell me about it, and he could not stand the embarrassment. I told him this argument merely attested to his lack of progress in analysis, because if he had gone far enough he would be capable of free association in which the patient can say anything, since the ego goals are set aside. (The ego goals are to avoid shame, guilt and anxiety.)

I resisted him because I knew his reason to be a rationalization concealing the underlying neurotic motive. However, I considered his request seriously, for whatever justification it might have.

I had a discussion with Barbara, and we agreed that after a few weeks we would tentatively terminate her visits to me. Barbara agreed to do this because she believed her husband's explicit promise that he would "sleep with her" if she didn't visit me.

I agreed because I believed that she had probably reached her maximum on the mental level, and if she could be complemented now by her husband's sexual activities she might react to them with enough mature love so that he would be interested in her again. The time had come, in brief, when I thought I had gone as far as I could with Barbara. Not that I was satisfied with what success had been achieved, but she had reached a point where she was attempting to control her husband through my offices. She wanted me to tell him what he could do and could not do, which, of course, was beyond my province. My observation told me that she was not only participating in the strivings and activities of her three sons, stimulating and promoting them, but she was also participating, on the unconscious level, in those of her husband. Indeed, some of her actions were driving him to commit the very acts she deplored.

In her dream life, in symbolic representations so disguised and distorted she could never interpret them, she took part in her husband's aberrations, even his sexual contacts with other women. Through these and other mechanisms, she was living out the impulses and strivings of her childhood, the most powerful of which was the drive towards reunion with her mother.

When Louis was in analysis with me alone, there was at first no change in his demeanor, his attitudes or his moods. He remained vague and stubborn. His business affairs and extra-marital activities were the subjects he dwelt upon exclusively. He never mentioned his wife's name. In his dreams, however, there were invariably a woman and another man beside himself. The predominant feeling was jealousy when the woman paid attention to the other man.

His primary need was to overcome the jealousy of having a man taken away from him by a woman, and he had to experience this pain-provoking situation over and over in order to build up immunity against the pain; otherwise the mortification of such an occurrence coming to pass again was a constant threat to him.

Actually he was not interested in having the man or the woman in his dreams for himself, but rather in overcoming the pain, fear and mortification of being abandoned by the man. In the course of the analysis, this was explained by an infantile experience. His father was taken away from him by what he imagined to be another woman when the father left his family in the old country to come to America and find a place for them. At that time a tension was set up in his unconscious mind, a yearning for his father which operated as incessantly as his life processes and had to be relieved constantly in his never-ceasing fantasies.

Louis' three sons were all father figures whom Barbara deprived him of by her mothering activities. He grew to hate her as the perennial depriver. This was his unconscious motive for getting Barbara out of the analytical situation. It was the same jealousy he felt when she began to gain strength and a measure of happiness through her analysis. Louis, in childhood, could only conceive that a strong and happy woman had taken his father from him. He had come to me to get back that father. When Barbara became stronger and happier as the result of her sessions with me, he had to get her out of the way, as though she were the strong, happy woman who took his father away from him in his childhood.

We say that water seeks its level, and that an ego goes back or retreats, but this is not so. Water does not "seek" and an ego does not "go." Both fall by the pull of gravity. Barbara's fixation in the field of time at the four-year-old level of make-believe, a base from which she had no capacity to lift herself, pulled Lou down to his previous levels of organization. Her effect on him was to prevent his thinking from materializing on higher levels of integration. As a consequence, there was no reality in Lou in which to live out his life. This unfortunate fate caused him to fall back into his fantasies, which reverted in time to his original objects—his parents. In that relationship, the most prominent feeling was the pain of having his father taken away from him. Since this husband and wife were both living in their infantile pasts, their adaptation to each other was necessarily of the primitive, archaic type. If she was this, he was automatically that. If she was strong, he felt weak. If she felt healthy, he was sick.

As Barbara began to regress after she was out of analysis for awhile, Lou started to make progress, and as he became more organized in his activity Barbara's demands for more progress on his part were markedly exaggerated. She was more disturbing than she had been for the past year, aggressive with her children, having temper tantrums, and exhibiting many of the old symptoms.

At Louis' suggestion, a three-cornered session was arranged. It was explained to Barbara how much improvement had taken place in Lou; how much more reality and promise he displayed in his planning for their future harmony and life together. But instead of being pleased and reassured, Barbara grew excited, pacing up and down the office, shouting threats at her husband and berating me for my failure not only with her but with him.

The more I tried to explain to her that it was obvious she was not pleased by her husband's improvement, the more excited and threatening she became. It was clear to Lou as much as to me that his recovery was causing a return of her sickness—a sickness that was part of the externalizations which were making a jungle of his home. Lou could see now that Barbara's sanity meant giving up his own soundness and mental health.

A week after this session, Barbara asked me for an appointment alone. When she came, she gave me an ultimatum. I had influence over her husband. I must tell him what to do instead of waiting until he grew up enough to be able to do as a husband should. By this she meant going to bed with her and having intercourse, giving up his carousing and ceasing to neglect his business.

She accused me of having "fancy ideas" about life and gave me an example of how she thought her husband ought to be dealt with. He had told her that once his father had forbidden him to go horseback riding, but he had gone anyway and got hurt. Then he had blamed his father for the injury, declaring that the father should have used force to keep him from going. Barbara agreed with that idea. She gave me one month to help her husband, herself and her children, and unless I took her advice she threatened to take matters into her own hands. I told her it was not my practice to tell people what to do, that it could only reduce an individual to obedience, and that in my opinion that did not lead to good relationships.

A month after the ultimatum, Barbara began to act out her threat. Lou appeared in my office with dressings on his face and a bandage on his hand as the result of an assault his wife had made on him. That day she had put his clothes outside the door of the house and wouldn't let him in, but agreed to meet him in his car. There she took out a strap with a buckle on it and beat him with it. He said she was like a wildcat; he could only barely defend himself.

As a result of this beating, however, he went home on time every evening. Her next move was to get rid of their twin beds and get a double bed. He slept in the double bed with her but kept to his side and still refused to have intercourse with her. One night she awoke at four o'clock and asked him to make love to her. When he refused, she began to claw at him. Before he left the house that morning, she opened the drawer of her dresser, and underneath her lingerie she showed him a long, sharp dagger and said to him, "This next." When I saw his wounds, I was more concerned than he seemed to be. He was surprisingly calm.

Shortly after she started on this new policy of force, I saw Barbara again. She told me I had a lot to learn about handling people, and what did I have to say about how she was able to get her husband to come home on time? I tried to persuade her to change her attitudes, in spite of what she thought she had achieved. I quoted to her the old saw her husband had tossed off as a warning: "You can lead a horse to water, but you can't make him drink." I attempted to show her that to subjugate someone by threat of force and violence was to instill fear and hatred.

But Barbara had tasted power. She had made contact with the three furies that live on the floor of all our personalities: the savage, the megalomaniac and the omnipotent infant. The jungle within her was now being externalized. She became her aunt—the witch, the hellcat. She was the torturer, and her husband and children were the tortured. We were back to the Barbara described to me by her sister-in-law, years before her analysis began.

On the other hand, Lou was becoming more sound and clear in his evaluations every day. He was, he said, living with a crazy woman, yet he couldn't bring himself to hospitalize her because then the world would know his sons had a psychotic mother. He couldn't take her children from her, because that, too, would raise many questions, and the boys would not want to leave her. She was the only world they knew, and if he tried to deprive them of her he could not foretell the kinds of violence that might ensue. But he was terribly worried about his sons, who he feared would become social cripples. What could he do to save them?

He went to their school and had long conferences with their teachers and the principal. He had fatherly discussions with the boys, in which his judgments, dispositions and advice to them were not only normal, but far more sympathetic and sound than one would find in the average father. The kind of soundness and sanity Lou was displaying seemed quite amazing. Finally, as a sort of coup, and out of his concern for the boys' welfare, he asked me to see his wife and himself once more at a three-cornered session, and I agreed.

During that hour, I witnessed an unforgettable spectacle. Lou began discussing his sons' welfare, his business and himself, while Barbara sat nervously pleating her handkerchief, her lips tight, her expression strained, her eyes flashing. If I could have excluded considerations of Barbara from my thinking, I would have approved her husband's grasp of reality.

Finally I turned to Barbara and said, "What do you think of all this?"

At that she loosed a barrage of vituperation, invective and accusations against her husband and me. She accused us of having engaged in a conspiracy against her. She asserted that her husband had ruined her life, and she had wasted three years on me. I had done nothing for her, and nothing for her husband; he was as bad as he ever was, even worse. It was impossible to reason with her or quiet her, much less give her any insight into her behavior. When they left the session, she stalked out with an attitude of high and mighty confidence. Lou followed with an expression of frustrated bewilderment and strained poise.

The struggle between this couple was not what it appeared on the surface. It really was a struggle for the higher levels of function in their respective minds. The goal they were battling for was rational life in a world of reality, and unfortunately, given their preconceptual aspirations, only one could win. It was a question of him or her. If he had beaten her up when she beat him, I think he might have saved her sanity, but at the cost of his own. Having accepted the humiliation of being the weaker one, he took away from her the opportunity of having a man for herself. Perhaps he would have envied her too much for having something of which he was deprived in his early childhood, something that lived on in him in his symbolic sphere as a perpetually recurrent yearning.

Without a man, Barbara was doomed to remain at the low level of sexual development at which she had been fixated. She had punished Lou enough to expiate his guilt, which had previously threatened him with imminent annihilation—a cure which illustrates the clinical fact that the schizophrenic psychotic who suffers a fractured leg may very well recover spontaneously from his psychosis.

Barbara, on the other hand, who had been doing the punishing, was building up a commensurate amount of guilt, and on the level of the unconscious it caused her constantly to anticipate retaliation. The more guilt she felt, the more defensive aggression she engaged in, and the more aggressive she was, the more her guilt mounted.

Obviously both these people had to use each other's symbol systems to dispose of massive quantities of riddance elements. What Barbara had to get rid of certainly could account for what happened to Lou and their children. What Lou needed to dispose of was, of course, far less malignant.

The goals I had set for dealing with the flaws in Barbara's character had not been achieved. The complication Lou introduced, interfering with the progression of her work, could not be avoided, for without a man to act as a husband to her, Barbara could make no further progress. Her only hope was for Lou to be able to see what held him back in his mental development.

At least their children now had one healthy parent, and the fact that the analyst did not appear to himself and to Barbara as the creative doctor he aspired to be was offset by the possibility that a more significant creative figure—the real husband and father of this family—might yet come to be.

The Jungle Within

Temporarily Lou was mentally sound. He appeared a reasonable human being, while Barbara seemed the dehumanized and dehumanizing one. What the future might hold for these people, no one could predict. Lou, however, was showing signs of genuine interest and responsibility for his wife. Perhaps this was more due to his love for his sons than to her appeal.

The sexual intercourse which she demanded and which he had begun to attempt continued to leave him feeling deprived and unsatisfied. Though she manifested a kind of satisfaction that should have satisfied him, it worked on him in the opposite way. This was explained to him as resulting from the fact that the fantasy of both of them was on the level of alimentary gratification instead of genital. Thus, according to the archaic alternative, if she was satisfied, he was not, and if she got what he wanted, he was deprived of it.

Lou's policy of let-well-enough-alone was being followed, day by day. But he was ready, and so was I, to do more creative work with Barbara if the opportunity should arise. Lou knew that the only way that his child-wife could become a woman would be if he could be a man for her and so feminize her, and it is my hope that this will eventually come to pass.

This, of course, means that he will engage her and awaken her sexually, so that she will achieve the fourth cardinal feature of aliveness, so that her mind will have the capacity of lifting her from her 4-year-old level to her current field of time.

Chapter 7

This Womb Is Temporary

People approach the natural world they live in by several pathways. To most it appears as extremely complex; yet the scientist who studies it is often surprised to find how organized and systematized it really is, and therefore understandable when it is studied. Many of those who are not scientists nevertheless approach the world intelligently and learn to cope with it and enjoy it. But at the opposite end of the scale exist those who live in a sleepy way in the great cradle of nature, bestirring themselves as little as possible, doing away with time.

These are the indolent and stagnant ones. Their enjoyments are misty, diffused and unformed. It is hard for the curious and discerning to understand what these others find so pleasurable in their nonemergence into reality. Their state could be termed "unbornness," perhaps, or "unexposedness." They seem incapable of venturing forth to go out and test the realities about them. They cannot endure the strain and pain of the elements and must withdraw to achieve for themselves the prenatal cushioning which means serenity and peace.

Such people live in dread of the original panic—that panic all human beings suffer at birth when they are suddenly and violently dispossessed from the haven in which they have known the undisturbed, completely peaceful existence. These are the unfortunate ones who were robbed of their God-given capacity to instrumentalize, to take initiative and build the apparatus to master the panic. They cannot relinquish the fantasy and the wish to return to the womb.

All this is illustrated in the case of Rosalie. I met her by a kind of planned indirection, as the result of a telephone call from a woman who was a friend of a former patient. She told me she had learned we were to be fellow guests at a dinner party that night, and had called to prepare me for an introduction to her twenty-one-year-old daughter, Rosalie, with whom she was having difficulty. She wanted me to meet Rosalie as though by accident, and to acquaint myself with her so that she could come to me eventually as a patient.

It is not my practice to ask questions or cross-examine patients or prospective patients. Rather, I go along with whatever they express, keeping my judgments to myself until these expressions are clarified. As it turned out, this mother's devious way of getting her daughter interviewed beforehand was typical of all her activities. Her behind-the-scenes maneuvers kept her daughter mystified and in the dark, never knowing what fate her mother was preparing for her, but always suspiciously anticipating something. Intrigue, plotting and planning constituted her way of life with Rosalie. It had begun even six months before the daughter's birth, when she had bought everything a child would need for years afterward—in anticipation of a boy.

My meeting with Rosalie went off well enough. She proved to be alert, inquisitive and engaging, and we were soon on the subject of psychoanalysis, about which she showed a keen curiosity. Rosalie's outward poise, the way she held her cup and used her fork, the way she chewed her food—all were perfect. I could only imagine what I later discovered to be hidden behind these exquisite manners.

Rosalie told me that she had thought of being analyzed because it would be "so educating," but in the next breath she declared that her mother had expressed the same view, and wouldn't it be interesting if they could both go to the same analyst. She asked me if it would be possible to do so. The mother, Rhoda, later asked me the same question, and it was plain that here was a silver cord situation and this kind of cord could not be easily cut.

I consented to having mother and daughter in analysis with me concurrently for a trial period of six weeks, after which I would give Rhoda an evaluation of what I thought about her and Rosalie and also give her some idea of what she could expect for the future.

At the time the analysis began, Rosalie was in a relationship with a man outside her faith and social stratum. (Rhoda, too, had married a man not of her faith.) Rosalie's friend, Bob, was an ex-GI who had had one arm amputated. He might have been sympathized with on the basis of his heroism, for he had been a hero, but he discouraged sympathy because he was a bitter-tempered, aggressive, sarcastic, ill-mannered boor. He had met Rosalie accidentally when her car ran out of gas, and he had pushed it to a service station. In no time they were dating regularly.

The relationship between these two had very soon become tempestuous. Somehow the most casual discussion between them turned into a violent argument involving their respective personalities. Name-calling, shouting and accusations would follow, and these fights would go on between them for hours at a time, ending at last in love-making. As the mother described what she saw of these scenes, "I was transfixed and paralyzed by fear of what would happen next between them."

This affair was disturbing the entire household. Rosalie was an only child and dominated her environment in her own way by the use of temper tantrums, followed by ventures into situations where she courted danger recklessly. She would drive her car at eighty miles an hour, or pick up strange men, or do other things calculated to frighten her parents.

Bob soon sensed the situation and grasped the opportunity to gain power over Rosalie, achieving the desired status by a shrewd, unspoken, subtle threat, which Rosalie sensed: he caused her to fear he might murder her, and therefore she had to appease him.

He strutted about, using their home carelessly and disrespectfully. Even when the parents were in the room, he disregarded them completely while he insulted Rosalie and on one occasion even slapped her in front of them. How it was that these parents could stand by while an outsider harangued, abused and slapped their daughter needs an explanation. They knew, said Rhoda, that any interference on their part with Rosalie's relationship with Bob would only have led to greater violence next time.

I asked how her husband could stand it and not do anything about it. Rhoda's voice filled with disdain as she exclaimed, "That husband of mine. . . ." The descending inflection was one of sewer-deep contempt. What she did not explain, and what I knew, was that this was one of the ways in which she and her daughter were able to demonstrate the complete degradation and impotence of the husband. If he had made a move in the direction of the young man, a threatening glance from Rhoda would have stopped him; a glance that would have said, You fool, don't you know that if you interfere with them Rosalie will never tolerate it? Here was the systematic diminution of the husband and father.

In the analysis, Rosalie insisted she was in love with Bob, even though it was not realistically understandable how a girl could be in love with a man who had no lovable attributes. Her neurotic needs, of course, were being served—needs that were unknown to her and could not be explained to her at the moment. She wanted to marry Bob, but it was my opinion that the marriage would be like a progressive disease for her. He was an affliction, and always would be to anybody with whom he was related. Yet I had to deal with the contention that Rosalie put forth in her own way: "People have no right to meddle with other people's love lives. It's something sacred, and others should keep out."

I knew she was using the word "love" to conceal other feelings of which she was not consciously aware. In her case, it was the need to experience over and over the fear of impending annihilation, and then to enjoy the pleasurable relief that it had not really happened. Her primary need was to defend herself against anxiety, which was rooted in a basic tendency to panic. Indeed, anyone who came along and knew in some hidden way how to frighten her could own her, and make her do anything he wished.

(A parallel case is the patient, sent to me by another psychiatrist, who thought she was entitled to a therapeutic abortion. The law in New York requires that before a woman may be legally aborted two doctors must testify that the life of the mother would be endangered by normal birth. When I interviewed this girl, she told me she had no idea why she had had sexual intercourse with the man who had impregnated her. She knew other men she liked better, and she had absolutely no interest in or feeling for this one. Relating what had happened between them, she told me he was an unimpressive man whom she had met casually at a party. While they were discussing the topics of the day, he had remarked that he could see nothing wrong with the acts of the men currently involved in the gang warfare known as Murder, Inc. If a man had to commit murder to get what he wanted, why not? The girl had no conscious knowledge of what effect his irrelevant remark had upon her, but beyond her awareness she feared he would murder her if she did not do as he wished, so she went to bed with him.)

Early in our sessions, Rhoda asked me if I knew a certain physician in New York. When I said I did, remarking that he was a famous and outstanding man, she asked in what was not really a question, "You know he's dead." I told her I knew that, and she added gleefully, "My germs killed him. When I went to see him a week before he died, I had a cold. He got it, and that was the end of him."

Rhoda was never direct in her threats nor in her derisive, disparaging or hostile remarks, but she would let one know constantly about the disfigurements, disasters and misfortunes that befell other people. She told me that before she married Rosalie's father three of her suitors had committed suicide, and she repeated this story many times. Rosalie had undoubtedly been so threatened by this mother, whose fantasies were constantly occupied with the destruction and disintegration of others, that the girl was in constant terror.

Bob was not the first of Rosalie's associations that were the result of her being possessed by fear. There was an affair when she was fourteen, and this, too, was with an amputee, a man named Mickie, who drove the grocery truck that brought daily deliveries to their country home. Mickie had a wooden leg. The analysis disclosed that this relationship was also the result of a subtle intimidation. One day, when Rosalie lifted a bag of groceries, she dropped a box of eggs. She pleaded with Mickie not to tell her mother but to take the blame for it himself. She showed such panic that Mickie came instinctively to understand that he could have absolute power over this girl.

The events in their relationship, which continued for two years, are too strange to be reported here. Rosalie insisted her mother knew what was going on, because whenever Rhoda saw Mickie, who was a married man in his twenties, she would give him admonishing sermons about what he should not do with young girls. Rosalie also insisted that on numerous occasions she knew her mother had not only detected them but spied on them. If this appears fantastic, it can only be added that Herbert, Rhoda's husband, always carried a pair of binoculars with him and used them to peep into other apartments when the family lived in the city.

It was another part of this strange picture that in Rosalie's early letters to her mother, when Rhoda was in Europe, she had drawn childish pictures on the margins, and all the boys who appeared in them had one amputated leg.

Rhoda gave lip service to letting her daughter live her own life, but she was constantly involved in all her activity, steaming open her letters and listening on an extension to her telephone calls. Both mother and daughter kept diaries which were secretly made available to, and read by, the other. The social amenities and courtesies were maintained between mother and daughter, but in reality there was a basic conflict of interests. Underlying hostilities and fierce antagonisms broke out frequently between them. In the fundamental sense, there existed between these two women the same deadly competition as between two sperm striving toward one goal. Without more reasonable developments and adjustments there could be no love between them, and it was clear to me that the mother's goal was not the protective one for her daughter that she had rationalized it to be.

But to go back to the beginning of the work, at the end of the agreed six weeks I gave Rhoda certain opinions. The analyst is realistic in his contemplations and anticipations of what will confront him on the road that leads toward his goals. One prediction to Rhoda was that her work with me would be hard and painful, because it would consist of travail that would be no less severe than that she experienced when she gave physical birth to Rosalie. The separation that would have to take place between Rosalie's ego and her own would be a complex and arduous task. Though she wasn't aware of it, on the psychic level they were like Siamese twins fused at the buttocks and head, and she herself would resist this separation as would such twins with the precarious implications of such surgery.

Ultimately, however, that would be the only way she could retain Rosalie, because if the taking away was not accomplished, eventually she would lose the girl completely to an institution, perhaps in two or three years, or else to some predator, or in some kind of catastrophic event.

I told her, too, that she would have to be ready for an apparent duplicity on my part, because I would appear to be against her. This duplicity was an expedient. I made it clear to both mother and daughter that it would be necessary, so that I could achieve the goals I had in mind. There was no other way. I would sympathize with the mother's point of view because of her basic needs, motives and drives, which were no more than strivings in her own behalf, for her own survival. But I would also see Rosalie's point of view because of her deep needs and strivings for her self-preservation.

As I explained to Rhoda, I was in this situation with objective interests, and these, too, were defined in no uncertain terms. The primary one, which she would have to accept consciously and accede to, was that Rosalie's mental health must take priority over everything else. Her maturity, independence and capacity to live her own life were the primary goals, to which all else would have to be subordinated, including the mother's comfort and happiness. I would carry on my own plans to bring about this achievement. The second goal would be to assure that Rhoda would have her daughter instead of losing her. As much as possible, Rhoda's interests and sensibilities would be regarded. Though I would seem to be exploiting her for the sake of her daughter, in the final analysis I would be contributing to her ultimate gain.

With these basic ideas understood and accepted, the work could progress, once I had a good enough hold of Rosalie's ego so that I was certain Rhoda would not be able to pull her away from me.

Herbert, Rhoda's husband, was completely dominated and overshadowed by his wife. I learned, as the analysis went forward, that

This Womb Is Temporary

Herbert was the second-born son of a prominent industrialist whose obsessive, compulsive drives in his business left no room for relationships with his sons in their early days. Herbert's bringing up was the sole responsibility of his mother, who was the giver, slipping him money under the table, so to speak, and giving him privileges that his father wouldn't know about with the implication that if his father knew, Herbert wouldn't be getting them.

When he was old enough to go into his father's business, he had to go through the same hardships that his father had gone through because the father believed this was the way to toughen him to make him capable of managing the business. What the father didn't realize, of course, was that while it had been intrinsic and appropriate that he battle his way out of the gutter, for Herbert, who had never built such conditioning, such a battle was destructive. Herbert became cowed and looked for a woman who was strong. When he met Rhoda he mistook her bluff, threat, and bravado for strength.

His position and importance in his daughter's life amounted to little or nothing. In Rosalie's dream production and associations, the representation in her unconscious of her father as an Oedipal figure was so dimmed by the wife as to be practically nonexistent, as though there had never been a father. Thus these two women were really relating to each other in an underdeveloped mother-child system of transactions. There were hardly any roots in Rosalie's basic personality structure that could be nurtured so that there would be room in her life for a male object. That was the extent to which Rhoda had extinguished the significance of her husband and had succeeded in keeping father and daughter apart.

When Rhoda discovered that she could not do with me as she had done with her husband—that is, control my thinking and lead me about by the nose—she was deeply shocked. This was a terrible threat to Rhoda and I could sympathize with her gathering anxiety.

In her own early days, her younger sister was the one whom her father called his beauty. Though Rhoda had devotion and love for her father, he overtly and crudely by-passed her but would compensate her by talking about her cleverness and shrewdness, and he very often slipped and called her his son.

157

Not infrequently in the analysis, Rhoda would slip and call Rosalie by her sister's name. In her unconscious fantasy, a father and daughter had to be kept apart by whatever means were available. It was therefore understandable that closeness between Rosalie and the analyst was a repetition of something that was unbearably mortifying. If she could frighten these two away from each other and intimidate them, there would be a place in the sun for her.

The first significant conflict came when I refused to forbid Rosalie to take a trip the girl had planned. By this time Rhoda realized I had won her daughter's confidence and could influence her, and she had become jealous of the position I had gained with her daughter and the position her daughter had gained with me.

I told Rhoda it was against my policy to make commandments, to forbid and impose my will on a patient. She tried to argue me into changing my mind, and when her arguments failed she began at first to whimper, then to cry, and at last she sobbed violently, entreating me to do as she wanted. When she found she could not shake my determination, she jumped up suddenly, rushed to the door, and, with primitive, threatening gestures and convulsive movements of her body, shouted at me that I would never see her again and she would see to it that our relationship would end.

In a firm and determined tone, I said to her, " Come back here and sit down." She did so with the calm submissiveness of an obedient child. Then I explained to her that crying is a power device, and that if I had been an ordinary man, her tears would have moved me to submit to her wishes, whether I were right, strong and clever, or the opposite. In fact, I said, as a man I felt for her and her suffering, but as an analyst I knew such tears had meanings and purposes. These were clearly defined in my mind, and if I permitted this device to influence my thinking and judgments it would do her no good. Ultimately, in such an event, I would simply be making it possible for her to defeat herself and allowing her unconsciously to interfere with her daughter's welfare and development.

So Rosalie went on the trip over her mother's objections and with the knowledge of her mother's behind-the-scenes futile attempt to enlist me as her tool. This was not the first time, of course, that

Rosalie defied her mother. In fact, defiance was the rule in their relationship, but it was the first time that her mother had failed to overcome a significant man in her life.

This defeat of her mother constituted a victory for Rosalie, not in the sense that a man was standing up for her, but that she was able to manipulate a man better than her mother.

My position in the lives of these two women was one which I had constantly to define and appraise—that is, to what purpose were they using me? What were their basic goals in this analysis? In the most elemental sense, their goals were antithetical to mine. Mine were to add to and endow them; their purpose was to subtract from me and to disendow me.

This deeper activity was completely belied by the surface attitudes of both. My disposition towards them had to be, and in fact was, friendly and sympathetic, even affectionate, as theirs was towards me, despite their unconscious murderous intentions. Rhoda was gross in her destructiveness and Rosalie was not so much subtle as she was timid, but in principle their goals were the same. In her dreams, Rosalie always used a man to destroy a man. For example, in one dream, she and Bob were climbing a hill. She handed a knife (a penis) to Bob (her tool) to plunge into a Chinese (the analyst) so that the analyst's creativity and masculinity would be undone.

Realistically and in the rational relationship we had, they did me no harm. Indeed, they were complimentary, looking to me for help. What greater respect could they give me? However, on the unconscious level of symbols they had to deprive me of my creativeness and my sexual identity to diminish or destroy me. This was their affliction. It had no effect upon me personally. I could only be understanding of what their sickness was and attempt to liberate them from it, to enable them to establish give-and-take relationships with a figure other than the image of the self—more specifically, with an object unlike the self. That would have to be a heterosexual object with whom they could achieve completion and so gain a life for themselves that could be perpetuated.

As time went on, it appeared that not only had Rhoda bitten off more than she could chew, but I had also. I had undertaken too much. There were old affiliations that Rhoda could exploit. She used her church in a way the church would never sanction, hiding behind its sanctuary and interpreting its forgiveness as a washing away of all her guilts, and manipulating sanctuary and forgiveness in such a way as to have the license to continue the very sins the church had forgiven. This is a common device used by some worshippers who think to hoodwink and outsmart God.

By these devices, the analyst's goals for her and her daughter's liberation were obstructed and his power was vitiated. One of the characteristics of Rhoda's sickness was the defeat of herself, and accordingly there was a powerful tendency to defeat the analysis that was attempting to stop her from defeating herself.

Analysis, as long as it is in process, meets resistance. The resistance is analyzed, and when it is overcome the patient is confronted by the anxiety the resistance was holding back. Then the anxiety is traced to its roots, and when and if the patient's conscious ego has become strong enough the root fear is automatically obliterated. Rhoda could not tolerate any anxiety without having to get the swift, magic relief to which she was conditioned from her earliest days. As a consequence, she could not face any problems at all.

She had still another powerful defense against anxiety. That was her reality, which she exploited in the same way that she used her church. This reality consisted of her marriage, her husband, the role of motherhood, her husband's name, and her father-in-law's importance in industry. All these were sources of spurious supplies to build her self-esteem so that she felt she could dispense with the analysis any time she wished.

In order to be effectual with Rosalie, the analyst had to be a potent influence. No sooner did she show signs of healthier relationships with healthier friends, and develop an interest in better things, than Rhoda would increase her subtle threats and intimidations. The mother did not intend to permit me to be more creative with her daughter than she was. At such times, resistances mounted, and what was produced in the sessions of both became more and more evasive and empty of content. These episodes were increasing in frequency and lasted a little longer each time. It was obvious to me that we had reached a stalemate.

It was then that I decided to make one more effort in behalf of Rosalie and her mother. I called for Herbert to come and see me. It was an ill-advised act. When Herbert came to my office, I spoke to him in the language of the layman.

"Your daughter needs a father," I said. "I cannot act as that father indefinitely. There is nothing I can achieve with your wife and daughter in analysis, but I can tell you what the basic trouble is. Your wife takes every opportunity to be the boss. She has to be the ruler of the universe, and Rosalie is waiting to take the same role when she gets the chance. Of course she will never have that chance as long as her mother is alive. There is only one chance for their normal development and that is for you to put your foot down."

The result of our conversation would not surprise any analyst. Herbert's reactions were accusatory. He told me that he had wasted his money and that I was walking out on my responsibility. He was terribly disappointed in me, he said, and then he began to rail against not only analysts and psychiatrists but the whole medical profession. Herbert was so frightened of his wife that he was unable to function as a husband and a father and a man. Faced with the necessity of doing so, he became completely disorganized.

Rosalie got away from Bob, but the relationships she developed afterward were no different in principle. Her role was to be the one who wore white gloves to show the world how pure her mother had made her, while underneath she was the low-grade woman her mother wanted her to be. In one dream wherein Rosalie aspired toward her analyst, she approached him with bundles in her arms. He told her to put down the bundles (they represented additional equipment she did not need in order to have a relationship with him), and she did so; but then she wallowed in the mud and filth all around her before she presented herself again to the analyst. The significance of this dream was that the analyst had to be turned into a mother figure, for whom she degraded and sullied herself so that the mother might have the feeling of purity, chastity and inviolateness.

But the analyst is not a perennial mother and does not profess to be one; therefore the analyst cannot condone, reassure, and love without contingencies. The patient has to do her part and grow up and be able to stand on her own feet and not be destructive against herself. Psychoanalysis is a scientific procedure, the purpose of which is to bring about maturity within a certain amount of allotted time. Although this time may vary by necessity, it must eventually come to an end. Rosalie and her mother would have gone on and on.

When the deepest roots that form the foundation of the personality have been sapped and softened and never allowed to grow and strengthen through initiative and activity, and the individual has been kept asleep by anodynes or an overprotective mother or equivalents so that he can't bear anxiety, he never develops sturdiness so that he may stand up independently to life. Rosalie's mother had never been allowed to develop such strength, never knew such strength and so couldn't deliver it to her child. If Herbert had himself not been so thoroughly incapacitated, he would have strengthened both of these females to be creative women instead of the self-defeating, male-envying, male-hating women they were. With them, the analytical process would have been unending. I could do no more for them. Accordingly, a six weeks' period was set to wind up the work.

Although this triangular analytical relationship did not materialize so that Rhoda's offspring could achieve emancipation, individuation and freedom, Rosalie's mind was sufficiently vitalized during the work so that she could begin to conceive of independent life.

About a year after the analysis terminated, Rosalie returned to me, alone, on her own earnings, and with determination to continue her personal analysis.

As she had in early childhood and all her life long, Rosalie had to reduce, deprive and break down the male object in whatever way she could. She instrumentalized infantile hatred as the force that would bring to her the previously known warmths which she had experienced in her earliest days, only from her father. Rosalie found it easier and safer to be hostile and destructive towards the father than towards the mother, not because the destructiveness and hatred toward the father were so great but because these feelings towards her mother were much greater and had to be completely repressed because fantasied anticipation of commensurate reprisal was too annihilating.

The brief contact I had had with her father and the three years of intimate association with her mother afforded me a kind of perspective and visualization in depth that may be compared with a stereoscopic view, so that I was able to guide this patient out of the dark labyrinth from which she could otherwise never have emerged.

With her mother out of the situation and no longer any communication through the diaries, Rosalie could relate to her analyst in a new way. After a year of work she was able to leave home and get an apartment for herself.

Rhoda's enterprise and activities with her daughter never changed in principle, but Rosalie was able to ward off her mother's symbolic and pantomimic communications so that they would not inveigle her into instinctual transactions that would keep her confined within her mother's orbit. Rhoda's curiosities, manipulations and intrigues continued, but Rosalie came to see them as symptoms of sickness. She became capable of understanding and forbearance towards her mother.

To the gratification of the analyst, the secondary goal and implicit promise to Rhoda that she would have her daughter was also achieved. Rosalie became an attentive and sympathetic daughter.

In one of her terminal dreams, a male friend loudly admonished her with, "Are you going to take such abuse from that old witch?" To which Rosalie responded, "I do not have to be affected by it or become excited over it. There is no point in hurting her. I am going to do as I wish anyway and she doesn't have to know about it."

The content of this dream clearly indicated that there was a sufficient amount of identification with her analyst so that she could treat her mother with humanness rather than by the retaliatory dehumanization which had, in the past, cost Rosalie her personal dignity and integrity.

Rosalie also came to see that to amputate an appendage from a male would, in reality, not afford her an additional appendage, and that symbolic realization on the basis of the archaic alternate—"if he hasn't got it, then I have"—was an empty illusion that added up to no natural sequences of life. Rosalie had furthermore to be the creator of her own way of life instead of living out the preordainments of her parents.

Rosalie's work, which lasted for three additional years after she returned alone, terminated successfully. Because her aims towards the male were no longer destructive, she was able to relate to him without anxiety, guilt and aggression, and to love and be loved.

Chapter 8

The Distorted Screen

On the mind's screen is the image of the self. It is an image projected from two directions, inside and outside. We come to see ourselves on this screen not only as we are but as others make us out to be. In the outside world are various projectors vying to possess and dominate the individual's screen with their particular kinds of picture. The mother may want to reflect one kind of image, the father another, and the church still another. The political system, too, has its own idea about what should register on the screen.

But there are forces from within which may also take possession of the screen—forces representing the characters that live on the floor of us. The way the individual conceives of himself in his body image is the way he is and does, but too often his vision of himself has been distorted and defiled by those who would capture the screen for their own selfish ends.

Such a distortion was clearly dramatized in the case of Lois, who was referred to me by another patient whom I had analyzed some years before. A model by profession, Lois was tall, slender, graceful and extremely beautiful. Her attractiveness was enhanced by the kind of charm exhibited by people who retain the winsome, wistful grace of a carefree child even after they have matured. She had, too, a quality infrequently found in people who begin analysis—that is, she was deferential, sympathetic and altruistic by nature. This kind of person says nothing without trying to measure the possible effect of his words upon the other person, to make sure that what he says does not impose upon or deal irreverently with the listener.

As I watched Lois' sensitive manner of listening for responses, preparing to see a point of view that was not hers, testing it and then accepting it fairly and reasonably, I considered her capable of the kind of sympathy characteristic of people who are adult enough to enjoy relationships of the loving and sharing type. Consequently, I wondered why she was in my office, but on the basis of years of experience I accepted her presence as an expression of a sickness known to her, and therefore I gave it credence.

Lois told me she wanted to be analyzed because she was "messing up" her life. She had reached a point, she said, where she felt a sense of danger so strongly that she was frightened into seeking help. Her immediate situation was an affair with the man who had referred her to me, full of the troubles and unhappiness arising from relationships in which people become progressively more intimate without being married.

It did not take me long to discover that Lois' altruism and sympathy were a thin veneer, artificially created by the clever and designing manipulations of her mother and developed quite simply for the purpose of attracting a rich man.

Lois was the second child of three siblings. Her father was the black sheep of rich parents, but not the one that strays from the fold. Living off the plenty about him, he was his mother's baby. Lois' mother married him because of the money in his family. She, too, was a beautiful woman who used her beauty for cold barter, and she hated her in-laws as the hungry infant hates its mother in an attempt to enforce supply. There was no subtlety about her demands and commands to "Fatso," as she and her children called the husband and father. She would say to him, "Those bastards are rich; go and get it."

Long before Lois began her treatment with me, her father's family had gone through their fortune; and since the father was not much of a breadwinner her mother had gone to work in a war plant. At the same time, however, she began drinking heavily and soon became an alcoholic, with all that constant drunkenness implies—screaming, violence, retching, sniveling, crying and neglect of her home. Her husband became the cook and cleaned the house and washed the dishes, while the children had to look after their mother, who was as helpless as an infant when she was drunk. After nine years of alcoholism, Lois' mother joined Alcoholics Anonymous and the situation was relieved.

Lois described her early life as though she were recalling a torture chamber. On the couch, she grasped her head, ran her fingers through her hair, sobbed and quaked as she told of the terrible humiliation of being hit on the head by her mother, of being slapped about so that she felt as though she were no more than a clod. Her mother's swift, devastating rages tyrannized her children and even her husband, who cowered in a corner until the tirades subsided.

"You'll never amount to anything," the mother would scream at Lois, banging the child's head against the wall because she had made a mistake in her catechism. "You'll end up in the gutter. You'll never be the beauty I am. You never had my beauty, and you never will." Her favorite threat was "I'll brain you."

By the time she was twelve, Lois was in trouble with nearly every male she saw. At thirteen, while her mother worked at night and her father in the daytime, she suffered a tragic and lustful experience at the hands of her father, an experience unforgettable and frightening. When she told her mother about it, the older woman used the information to terrorize both husband and child. First she told her husband's parents, ranting and screaming about it for everyone to hear.

When the mother became blind drunk, she would crawl into bed with Lois, tell her how much she loved her and how she was her favorite child, and attempt to hug and kiss her. At these times, Lois was terrified and pushed her mother away, because she knew there was something in her behavior that was unnatural. Later, when Lois attended meetings of Alcoholics Anonymous with her mother, she saw similar intimacies carried on with the mother's many girl friends.

Frequently Lois had to drag her mother out of some saloon, paralyzed with drink, and such terrible shame overwhelmed the child that she ceased to care whether she lived or died. Once, while the mother was drunk and driving the car, she threatened, "If you kids don't shut up, I'll drive this car off the bridge." Lois thought what a good thing that would be and hoped she would.

Lois' earliest reactions were defiance and rebellion. Though she was physically slight, she became the fighter of the family. Her role was to protect her brother, two years younger, against the tough kids of the neighborhood. Her older sister had allowed herself to become so dominated by the mother that she had completely surrendered initiative. She was retarded, withdrawn, mutistic and dull in her thinking, doing whatever her mother said, offering no challenge and therefore offering no target. The younger brother had also surrendered, becoming dull and flat, taking to beer drinking in his early teens. He sipped away at it slowly but constantly, virtually to the exclusion of solid food.

The father, too, submitted completely and literally hid in a corner of the house. He brought home his pay check from a factory job, and his wife gave him an allowance. However, he was not the helpless character his attitude and the derisive nickname of "Fatso" implied. When he was crossed, his foot would spring out to strike anybody, anywhere—in the belly, the shins, the head, the genitals. But unlike his wife he was remorseful and penitent after his rage was spent and tried to make it up to the victim.

Lois herself was defiant and struck back at anyone who threatened either her or her sister and brother. She had a strong sense of justice, identifying with the underprivileged and with animals. Whenever her father kicked out at a dog, she got into a battle with him, calling him a "dirty murderer."

Her defiance of her mother manifested itself in masturbatory activity, which her cousin taught her when she was about seven years old. She indulged in this with complete abandon and with no conscious shame or guilt. She even tried to teach her sister, telling her it was thrilling, but her sister was afraid.

When Lois went to confession she told lies, and when she pretended to put money in the box she stole a half-dollar instead. But she would say in her mind, "God, I'm just borrowing this. I'll give it back to you." Then she skipped down to the store and got an ice-cream soda. She was almost obsessed with ice cream, and even while she was in analysis she could eat a quart of it at one sitting. If anyone tried to take a spoonful from her, she would react with more violence than as if he had tried to take her valuables.

At five, Lois knew her catechism by heart and she was the nuns' pet. In analysis she repeated the catechism, but she had not the slightest notion what any of it meant, nor had she ever known. As a child, she recalled, she had examined the crevices on the soles of her feet to see what the sins of her soul amounted to.

All these occurrences had resulted in the strange and complex mixture the analyst learns to know as he observes the crucible in which influences, attitudes and dispositions are deposited and combined with each other. In defending herself against the terrors of her mother, Lois became her mother, adopting her aggressiveness as her own defense. She became a fighter like her mother, so that when she was sixteen and her mother lashed out at her with her fists, Lois struck back and gave the older woman such a beating that she never laid hands on her daughter again. But it was also through this identification with her mother that Lois became energetic and enterprising. By the time she came to me she was a high-priced model, earning more than many a successful professional man.

Although the disciplinary brutalities of her mother left Lois with feelings of shame, degradation and humiliation, and she had active resentments and hatred of her mother, nevertheless she felt a sense of duty and responsibility. Her dream was to give her mother everything she wanted and to have her family as tranquil as other families she knew. Although she wanted to escape her home and be free of it, she was tied to it because she had been so intensely indoctrinated by her mother.

This indoctrination was the result of constantly repeated old saws: "Blood is thicker than water. . . . No one will ever be to you what your own will be. . . . A mother is the only friend you have in the world; outsiders are outsiders." The mother bound Lois to her by the daughter's sense of guilt; she complained bitterly about how her children had ruined her life and made a slave out of her and robbed her of the chance of having fun. Motherhood, she often said, was like being in prison. Only Lois could save her.

In spite of her beauty the mother had never achieved any success on her own, and she did not train Lois for the kind of success her daughter achieved. In fact, it could be said that Lois achieved it in spite of her mother, who specialized in aggression. Sexuality in this family was completely suppressed, and Lois' anatomy was utilized as a commercial commodity. Her indoctrination early in life took the form of, "Get your foot in his belly before he gets his foot in yours." When Lois was younger, her mother would say to her, much as she had said to her husband, "They are rich; take it from them." When she and Lois were in a department store, she would say, "Do you like that article on the counter?" If Lois said yes, the mother would motion with swiftly shifting eyes, as though to say, It's all right. Nobody is looking; take it. And Lois would take it. Thus her mother had another whip to hold over the girl's head.

When Lois began to earn big money as a model, she spent it on her family much as though she were the husband. Her sense of obligation to them was overwhelming.

The unique and conspicuous fact about this young woman's history was the discrepancy between her two ways of being. On the one hand, she was an adorable, cheerful, three-year-old child, and on the other, she was a hard, sophisticated, knowing model. Her fantasies, however, were those of the three-year-old. They always began with being in the toilet, and the greatest thrill came when the door opened and outside were innumerable bottles of Coca Cola and ice cream cones.

Her sexuality was nothing more than the machine-like acting out of words and learned activities that were not felt as erotic or emotional experiences. She was completely unawakened, which is to say that she was completely repressed. Her virtue was easy but it was not men as such that interested her. She wanted to achieve life for herself by possessing her mother. As a matter of fact, she had to degrade men.

"It really doesn't matter who the man is," she told me, "as long as I can get him hot, bothered and excited, and then when he is at the peak of his excitement I drop him like a hot potato and watch him suffer. The thrill comes only when I see him miserable and disappointed, weak, foolish and begging. To hear a man cry that he doesn't know what to do next, that's what I really enjoy." She added earnestly, "But don't misunderstand me. I like men."

Whenever she approached a man in her dreams, another woman —an older woman—was always there, casting a forbidding glance at her and saying, "He'll make a fool of you. He'll ruin you and leave you. He wants only one thing from you, and that's what they all want. He'll leave you in the gutter."

In one session Lois talked about her fantasy, or wish, to be the most beautiful woman in the world. When I asked her why she wanted to be the most beautiful woman in the world, she told me it was because she could then (in her fantasy) sit in a room while a million men marched by in single file, and as they looked at her they would drop dead. This fantasy clearly indicated that she visualized her whole being as a power device to destroy all other sperm, so that she would have no competition in her aspiration to achieve the ovum—the mother—a life.

Such total asexuality could be readily ascribed to the terrifying sexual experience she had endured at the hands of both her parents. The men with whom she consorted were, for the most part, smart young advertising men whom she chose for the amount of money they had to spend. They were as prankish in their interest as she was. Their bold, brave sexual talk and doings amounted to practically nothing.

Lois had one great need. That was to be told she was beautiful and told it over and over again. When she was a child, in her spite and rebellion and bitterness, she had sometimes looked into the mirror and told herself how beautiful she was, and kissed herself in the mirror. That was her childish attempt to try to convince herself that she was not as ugly as her mother made her feel. But even now she couldn't believe it, no matter how many times she heard it, and notwithstanding that she earned her living by it. She changed the color of her hair frequently, and there were not enough dresses for her to buy. She primped constantly, using eye makeup and lipstick to excess. This was because in her unconscious mind there was a clear picture on her screen, projecting itself into her physical being as her mother had arranged it. The picture showed her as something ugly. Moreover, the degradations, the inferiority, the worthlessness impressed upon her made it impossible for this truly beautiful and delightful girl in her conceptions of herself to register anyone's sincere recognition of her, so completely had her designing mother won the screen of her mind.

Equipped with my knowledge of Lois' case, there were two things I had to do for her. One was to wage war on this powerful mother and win away from her the screen upon which she projected the fraudulent image of Lois that was depriving this young woman of the right to see herself as she was, truthfully and naturally. I did not doubt that this would be a monumental task, because the instinctual tieup on the deepest levels of amalgamation are so inclusive and intertwined that it would be complex and precarious to separate this daughter from her mother.

My second task was to re-educate her about men. Her father was not much of a man; he was merely a tool for Lois' mother to use for her purposes, which were primarily to do whatever she could to him that would accrue to her personal advantage. Such a tool, used for ignoble purposes, comes to have ignoble characteristics and to be thought of as contemptible. Indeed, one's own contemptibility may be released or unloaded through it. One achieves mastery or control over what one unloads or has to unload, and such a riddance brings about a state of relaxation similar to that we achieve by overcoming anything that may threaten us, namely, guilt, tension or anxiety.

And so, to Lois a man was someone to gain access to for the purpose of unloading contemptibility, anxiety and guilt. A man might gaze at her, adoring her beauty, remarking about it, glowing with it, but all this culminated invariably in her mastery of him because of the susceptibility of his mind to the dictates of his genitalia. Then she would make him into her own, to utilize for her own unloading fantasies. Such relationships relieved Lois of her anxieties and guilts, but they did not relieve her of her reactions to herself—her feelings of unworthiness, pessimism, homeliness and aloneness.

Lois' relationship with her analyst was unique in one significant respect, that is as far as her relationships to men were concerned. In my natural, yet studied, reaction to her she could register, and was caused to register, that I had noted her beauty and remarked about it with appropriate words. The effect on her was as negative as she had ever experienced before; however, she held in fantasy the latent hope that ultimately she would control, master and degrade her analyst as she had other men.

The analyst, of course, is well aware of such drives, and is equipped to deal with them. Not being able to gain access to him through his carnal nature, and therefore not being able to unload, Lois was left with the anxieties that kept her striving. This anxiety supplied the energy for a good deal of the work that had to be done, to build out of the lower-level elements the higher centers essential for better realistic adaptation.

Lois was admirable, beautiful and lovable in the eyes of her analyst. He would have been expressing an untruth, and in her instance a malignant one, if he had been compelled to blind himself defensively against the impulses such beauty would arouse in any man. But in these situations the analyst's attitude is that of a grown-up, cultured, socialized man who knows that to look at a thing of beauty does not mean he has to touch it or become intimate with it. He discerns, evaluates and enjoys it for what it is without participating personally in its just privacy and integrity. It was even more than usually essential in Lois' case to maintain the respect afforded any patient, to establish the same dignified and integrated distance that parents should, socially and naturally. Patient or child then has the opportunity to evolve and become psychosomatically-sexually mature in his own behalf, then go on to mate and make his own independent life and family.

On this basis, I could wage a battle against the predatory mother who had deceived Lois, defrauded her of the simple and elementary truths about herself, and bound her through lower-level, instinctual, libidinal attitudes. She also had to be freed from the father who had trapped her in early life, binding her to him excessively.

Lois wanted to repeat her early experiences over and over again with her analyst. This was her instinct, which was identified with basic aliveness. If forfeited, it would forfeit simultaneously the aliveness itself with which it was identified. These were the old attachments. But the higher cultivation for which we were striving in the analysis—that is, developments within her highest spheres of thinking—would give her the ability to integrate and measure time, to differentiate between the current, future and past fields of time. In these higher areas, there is the functional capacity to overcome the pull of gravity and lift ourselves to the "now" of our lives.

Because Lois wanted her analyst to criticize her, she gave him every opportunity, tempting him in the most subtle ways to deprecate, degrade and humiliate her and to punish her with his psychic riddances. She went to great lengths, becoming extremely aggressive on occasion. She threatened, taunted and dared the analyst to punish and hurt her. But her efforts were unflinchingly analyzed for their meaning and purposes. When she failed to get from her analyst the releases of the tensions automatically springing up in her unconscious mind, she tried to get from him what she had gotten from her father; but this, too, was analyzed and described in its meaning, origin and motives.

Always she was reassured that, on the level where we were originally committed and dedicated, her analyst would never forsake her. He would also never compromise the original understanding that her goal was to be mental maturity and the full growth of her emotional capacity to make a life for herself, free and belonging to her own future, rather than to have her prerogatives usurped by one who had been given an opportunity to help and had selfishly taken advantage of her.

The goal of the analysis was clear, and Lois appreciated it and grew up to it. Because she had this new experience she was able to relinquish the one that bound her to the old image projected on the screen of her mind—the image that was a lie and a distortion.

The unmasking of the big lie drove a wedge between her and her predator. It was anticipated that when Lois began to be able to defend herself against the degradations her mother heaped on her the mother would find other means to break her down. All predators, particularly inferior ones, have to subordinate the ones they intend to exploit. They must find ways of reducing their victims in their own estimation, in order to force them to carry out the exploiters' wishes. The mother had to do this to Lois to keep her under her thumb and so retain her as the breadwinner of the family.

When Lois came to realize that it was no "disgrace," as her mother had taught her, to think about and take care of herself, she began to conserve herself for her own life and not sacrifice herself and her self-esteem and surrender her earnings for a family which should have been looking out for itself.

Her father's reaction to Lois' new self-interest and self-assertiveness was approving, but her mother was guarded at first. She used subtle devices, which became less subtle as time went on, to remind Lois of how she used to shoplift. She also reminded her daughter about an abortion Lois had had. All of these activities were designed to produce feelings of guilt and shame, the devices her mother could manipulate and so continue to hold Lois in bondage. These were translated in the analysis so that she could recognize her mother's tactics and over-all strategy, which were to make her into a subjugated servant so that her mother would be secure for life.

Lois was warned that her mother would take to drink again as a last-ditch stand, to keep the daughter from freeing herself. This would be a powerful threat to frighten Lois away from her newly found gains of normal social thinking and adjustment. The prediction proved true. Her mother did begin to drink again, but by this time Lois was prepared to be unaffected. Without the work of the analysis, this would have been the intimidation that would have caused Lois to capitulate. When her mother saw that Lois paid no attention to her drinking, that it meant nothing to her, she was more amenable to the financial settlement of a hundred dollars a month her daughter offered, with the proviso that if she did not behave herself Lois would withdraw the support and wash her hands of the whole family.

Before concluding this case, I would like to make clear that in the tremendous task of freeing Lois from her mother I was aware that the task of rehabilitating such an individual is extremely difficult. When certain injuries and deprivations and rejections occur in the earliest days, and the predators have gained ingress to the very roots of the individual's being, defenses against anxiety and panic are flimsy.

The task did not, however, turn out to be so monumental as I had thought. This was because of the help of Fred, the man who had sent Lois to me originally. It is not often that an analyst has available a reality in which the patient can test for himself the new insight resulting from his analysis. Fred's deeper appreciation of Lois and her struggle against her old ties, and his visualizations of her potential, made him patient, sympathetic and supporting.

When the unreality is analyzed and the neurotic defenses are taken away from an individual, he does not want to surrender them unless a better alternative is offered. That he should give up one system for no system at all is hardly to be expected. But when a new system that is better than the old is in readiness, it is reasonable to suppose that the individual will want to make the shift.

Lois had a reality to turn to with Fred. Now she did not have to live in the present with him with the emotions that had to do with the past. She could relate to Fred, who loved her and wanted to give her a life, have a family with her, build a future with her, and have their own descendants. But without her comprehension of the respective spheres of time, she could not have released herself from her old ties to yield herself to him and to their future.

$\mathscr{S}\mathscr{S}\mathscr{S}$ Book Three

Chapter 1

The Analyst and the Children

Rarely does the child of neurotic parents get a sympathetic hearing. Generally speaking, grownups are not as interested in children as they pretend to be. We are prejudiced against them, or rather against the child who lurks in the foundations of our own personality, so we project and say, "What a brat that child is!" And how often have you heard parents exclaim, "I can't wait for the camp season to start!" We disidentify with children in order to identify with the society of grownups, and in doing so we often become pompous, arrogant and overserious. Youngsters refer to us as stuffy.

On the other hand, some of us are anything but prejudiced against children. We overidentify with them and go to the other extreme by satisfying their every wish, overloading them with supplies, overprotecting them, and practically suffocating them with love and demonstrativeness. We are not aware that what we are really trying to do is to compensate ourselves for the lack we suffered in our childhood, to repair our old wounds, and to make laboratories out of our children in which to find the solutions to our own neurotic problems and satisfy the unappeased hungers of our own childhood.

It is hard for people who overidentify to accept the fact that although they get vicarious gratification in a substitute, symbolic way when they shower their children with love and pseudo-altruism, at the same time they envy them on the unconconscious level for getting what has been denied to them. In fact, on this level, they hate the children for it.

The children of such parents sense this. They are not fooled by rationalized justification for the excessive and unnecessary cruelties of training procedures, for the sadisms involved in punishments (to teach), or the humiliations and degradations contained in the teasing and fun-making of guffawing grownups who honestly believe they are being tender and loving in such relationships. Worse, children know and feel that they are being used by such parents, and they get to feeling "left out," as indeed they are. The reality of their lives, their needs and feelings remain unrecognized. They feel uncared for, unprovided for and unprotected. There are toys galore, stores of food, overloaded wardrobes, nurses and tutors—but no mother to love the children. Mother loves exclusively the child that she is herself.

Children in this situation have sad, pained faces, and eyes that are overalert and quick. Where one would expect to find the shine and confidence of optimism there is the dullness of futility. They never utter a word about the woe that hangs over their lives, because no words really are adequate, and if any existed there would be no one to listen.

A child is a privately owned being. The way he is owned is as varied as the constellations that surround him. Often being owned to the exclusion of self means he is merely the instrument by which the parent achieves satisfaction. Later he continues to be the means by which other people are satisfied at his expense.

If the father and mother have an unconscious need to wish their child to be the unhappy one, the pained and deprived one, the one who is commanded to "be less than I am," the child has no alternative but to comply. Then he grows up and reaffirms the parents' original wish or dictum, continuing to be the person his parents made him be. In fact, when a parent in analysis comes to see what he is doing to his child that he didn't know he was doing, and then changes his way, the child will force the parent by attitudes and maneuvers into previous aggressive acts. Moreover, when that child grows up, as I have observed and ascertained, he will continue to affirm and re-affirm the parents' original will and either find an actual punishing, depriving object for himself or else create one.

I do not contend that the grownups of such neurotic families are guilty of cruelties and indifference to children, any more than they are guilty of ridding themselves of used-up, unneeded and other worthless elements. They are simply disposing unconsciously of what threatens them in their symbol system, and therefore they are morally and spiritually innocent of the harm they do to their children.

Fortunately there is an entirely new factor in the lives of such children today: the psychoanalyst. Because of his special training and scientific knowledge, he can listen to them sympathetically and allow them to make the words that will tell their tale of woe and get help. Although there may be resistance in the beginning, no parent I have ever analyzed was ungrateful for being made to know consciously what he had been doing unconsciously. Parents need their happy and healthy children as much as they need their own dear lives. The new knowledge they acquire through the subjective search breaks the chain of events that caused them to transmit automatically through the unconscious into the symbol systems of their children those insults and injuries they received at the hands of their forbears. Higher-level realizations show the parent that, realistically, he does not become bigger by making his children smaller, nor himself better by making his children worse. Such archaic relativisms are no more than the shadowy interplay of symbols and have no reality in man's corporeal being.

Several years ago, I made an analysis of a child who was presented at a clinic. His case demonstrates clearly what tragic situations parents can wander into when they cannot see where they are going, and what catastrophic events can occur because they have no knowledge of the natural body functions and processes of their evolving children.

It was 12:30, and the regular Friday conference was in session. The case was that of a five-year-old boy who had set fire to his brother's crib. Before his mother could get to it, the baby had burned to death. Jimmie was to be questioned by the psychiatrists, psychologists and psychiatric social workers attending the conference. The little patient sat quietly in his chair, looking around casually at the specialists who were sitting in rows before him. He seemed unconcerned; perhaps he was wondering what all this had to do with him.

"Did you set fire to the bed?" asked one of the psychiatrists. There was no accusation or blame in his voice.

"No," Jimmie answered. His voice was disinterested, and his expression was as peaceful as that of a contented, comfortable, sleeping child.

Yes, he liked his brother, he explained to another psychiatrist, and wanted to go home and play with him. Was there a fire? He didn't know anything about it and appeared not to believe it. What were they talking about, anyway? He wanted his mommy, and when was she coming?

But according to the history given by his mother there was no doubt about what had really happened. The folder of matches that was on the kitchen table had disappeared. Jimmie had been in the kitchen, walked out, returned again, and was playing with his fire engine when she smelled smoke and rushed to the bedroom to see the crib in flames.

Jimmie's denial was complete, not only to his audience but to himself. Technically, we were witnessing the phenomenon of repression; the memory of the event was gone, excommunicated. It was too painful and thus it was disowned, as it were, by his community of associated ideas. Nature had come to his aid as it would have if a thorn had penetrated his skin, when a wall of defense would have been built immediately around the foreign and unwanted mass, which would be kept outside the body substance proper and eventually pushed out.

Jimmie showed no evidence of guilt. He did not remember doing anything and consequently had nothing to feel guilty about. To him, nothing had happened. Told that his brother was dead, and that he would never see him again, he answered calmly, "Oh, yes, I will. When I go home, I'll see him."

"But he's dead and they've taken him away," he was told.

"He'll come back," Jimmie answered confidently.

It would have been easy to call the boy a liar, but that would not have been true. He believed what he was saying. He was not falsifying the reality as it existed within him, so his communication was honest. The only reality any of us know is that which occurs through registration within us, so when Jimmie asserted his brother would return even if he had died he believed it. To a child of his age, death is reversible; he can make believe and believe what he wishes. Accepting the idea that the dead can come alive again is easy for him.

Nevertheless it was true that Jimmie had killed his little brother. Why had he done it? We could theorize about it and reconstruct what might have happened to make him perpetrate such a thing. Children do burn themselves when they play with fire, and with some the memory of the burning is felt clearly and continuously. A child of this age also plays with himself, and a mother, frightened by this masturbatory activity, could be impelled to "save him from himself," to frighten and punish him.

When Jimmie played with fire, he was burned and thereafter he avoided it. What has that to do with playing with himself? In self-play, there are excitement and increased body heat, which, in his misty thinking, he associated with the heat of fire or the fire itself. Thus playing with himself and playing with fire became similar, in that one reminded him of the other. Both were felt as heat; both had the feature of bringing painful consequences. Both were pleasurable, and both were followed by pain, fright and bodily injury. Jimmie did not want to suffer these effects, so instinctively he sought to avoid the causes. Fright sets up a fear mechanism. Fear is a defensive signal that recurs automatically to alert the human organism to avoid pain and bodily injury.

Getting burned by fire was not a problem for Jimmie because fire was an outside occurrence and the threat of it could be discontinued. All he had to do was not to play with it. But what about the punishment, fright, pain and bodily injury that were caused by playing with himself? The threat of that could not be discontinued. The urge to play with himself recurred as naturally and inevitably as thirst and hunger, but no sooner did the urge appear than also occurred the anxiety warning him of the consequences.

Now he was really in trouble, constantly threatened by imminent danger. He could not hear, see, smell, touch or locate the cause of his anxiety, and he did not know what was threating him, but he felt the unease, the tensions and the discomfort of it. He had to do something to relieve himself. He could not reach inside to uproot the throbs and impulses at their root so that he would not have the urge to play with himself. There was no avoiding it; the threat was constantly upon him.

Jimmie strove to survive, and nature came to his aid. Being human, he was endowed with a rationalizing apparatus, so he could rationalize his urge to play with himself. On the more primitive levels of thought, a part of a thing can resemble the whole, or one thing may resemble another and produce similar effects. The heat produced during the excitement of self-play was associated and identified with the heat of the fire. To avoid one, then, would be the same as avoiding the other.

Now he could externalize his problem to the world of reality where he could cope with it—that is, he could set a fire, and by putting it out he would believe he had snuffed out the urge to play with himself. Thus Jimmie found the way out. Following his instinct to defend himself against what threatened him, he set fire to his brother's crib. Seeing the fire happening to someone else proved it was not happening to him, and perhaps even that it would never happen to him again.

It is possible of course to suppose that Jimmie was malevolent toward his little brother under the cloak of benevolence, giving him the pleasure of playing with himself and getting excited and heated, but all the time planning to make him the burned, punished and injured.

It may even be argued that he was attempting to protect his brother from such suffering. He was playing with his fire engine when his mother smelled the smoke, and fire engines are made to extinguish fires, not to start them. Consequently it may be surmised that his intention was to set the fire for the purpose of extinguishing it. However, I do not believe this was the case. He was only trying to survive, as any of us would do, trying to deal with his own urges, attempting to block and extinguish them at the source so they would not impel him to the physical activity, with its inevitable concom-

itant, anxiety, which theatened imminent suffering. He had ɪ
awareness of what he was doing to his brother than a chɪ
pushes aside an obstacle standing in his way as he heads to·
goal.

But if Jimmie was so innocent, why did he have to repɪ
memory that he had set fire to his brother's crib? When he hɛ
mother's screams of pain and horror, which he identified wɪ
felt as his own, he ascribed it to the fire itself, as though
burned her. Then it had to be gotten rid of and completely reɪ
because a threat to his mother, the agency through whom
ceived his vital supplies, was a threat to himself. Jimmie
wanted to get rid of the threat to his survival. We cannot
him for this, nor for wanting to be without pain. This is wɪ
all want. There is no need to forgive Jimmie; he doesn't need
was able to prove to himself and the world that he had done n
wrong. We needed only to look at him to see how innocent h

The major question remains, however. What can we do,
sponsible adults, about such a tragedy? Certainly not walk awɪ
do nothing. A terrible sense of frustration would be certain tɕ
take us. When such a wrong takes place, it is only human
something to right it. But if we punished Jimmie it would
though we were punishing the innocent, and we would be lefɪ
the feeling that we were merely being revengeful or cruel.

What about his mother? Was she guilty of a crime of omɪ
that of leaving the matches where Jimmie could reach them
more significantly, of failing to understand her child? What
would it do to punish her? Would punishment enlighten
Punishment only makes an individual afraid of more punishɪ
and we have already seen in Jimmie's plight what devious co
can be taken and what disastrous consequences can result wh
way out of expected punishment and injury is sought.

Jimmie cannot be punished for the crime, nor can we undɕ
death of his brother. The only thing we can do is to understand
it happened, so that it will not be necessary to grope in the dar
Jimmie did. We can try to enlighten his mother, or any mothe.

that more will be known about the way a child feels, thinks and has to act.

Jimmie wanted primarily what we all want—to survive and to be without pain. He had to disown the pleasurable activity and experience of masturbation because of the injuries that followed. It was natural and healthy for him to want to have pleasurable activities and experiences, and to avoid pain and injury as well. If his mother could only have known that when Jimmie was playing with himself he was doing no differently than any child his age would do quite naturally. If she could only have trusted that nature has its own ways of defending a child, and that his God-given regulators, working as automatically for him as his own heartbeat, could not possibly work in such a way as to be detrimental to him. If only she could have known that within six months or a year this self-play would cease and then he would be in his latency period, during which time his sexual energies would be utilized and consumed by the processes that would socialize and educate him.

If his mother could have observed his natural activity and not interpreted it as evil or unnatural, she might have let him alone, and if she had, he certainly would have let his little brother alone.

This tragic story is a glaring example of commonplace forbiddance. It is told here to emphasize the sequels of ignorance and of blindness to simple and elemental instincts in children. We do not see or understand these instincts because they are obscured by a curtain made up of fables, jargon, high-sounding words, prejudice and ignorance, which screens reality from our natural perceptions. It is an enormous task to persuade human beings to unlearn the superstitious mumbo-jumbo that frightens them and that they live by, so that there can be room in their mental apparatus for a few truths and plain facts about themselves and their children.

Another illustration of these truths is the case of Kate. It was to be expected that the daughter of Della, one of my patients, would inherit the pains, insults and degradations Della herself had endured at the hands of her own mother. To understand the developments that took place in Kate's life we must look back into Della's life

experience with her mother. Once the child's fate would have been called "pre-ordained," but actually her sickness was related directly to her grandmother. Della had to reconstruct her mother in the vehicle that was her child in order to overcome the bleak, hollow echoes reverberating out of her symbol systems, making her feel empty and worthless.

It is a commonplace to hear a mother make some such empty threat to her child as, "I'll bash your brains in." There are children, however, who are more impressed than others by these threats. The child whose mother hasn't warmed it, caressed it and loved it is more devastatingly affected than others. To him, such threats are possibly imminent occurrences, and he grows up to have as much panic as though the threats were going to be made good at any moment. Before she came into analysis with me, Della discharged onto little Kate the same kind of material in the same sudden frenzies that her mother had discharged onto her.

Kate was four years old when her mother came under my care, but by that time the groundwork for her breakdown had been laid. At the age of seven, the child's flimsy and precariously constructed ego collapsed, and she suffered a serious break with reality. A change came over her. She complained to her mother that her classmates were ganging up and planning to make her fail in her work so that she would be thrown out of school. She said her teacher chose her to be asked the kind of questions that couldn't be answered, and thus she was shamed in front of everyone. She was having nightmares, and even when she was awake she thought thieves were coming in the window and feared they would shoot her. She was in such a panic over all these threatening situations that she had to stand three to six feet from people she talked to for fear they would do something violent to her. Sometimes she would throw at them whatever was in reach.

Thoughts came into her mind that she did not want. Sentences formed themselves on her lips that she did not want to say. She said to her mother, "I have to say that I hate you. I don't want to say it, mother dear, but I have to. I hate you and I wish you were dead. I wish Agnes [her younger sister] was dead, too, and I hate her.

Mother, can't you stop these thoughts from coming into my mind? I hate the thoughts."

Kate was also frightened about what she imagined was happening to her body. Materials were accumulating in her ears, she thought, and she was terrified by the idea of removing them. She felt that something was growing in her abdomen. Her most terrible fear was that she would see vomitus.

She accused her mother of being false. "The things you say, mother, and the expression on your face—they're all lies about what you really feel for me. You hate me."

When they brought her to me, Kate was in such a state of agitation that I had to resort to a procedure rare in my work. I had to administer seven electric shock treatments to erase completely much of the material that normally belongs to unconsciousness but in this child had broken through and appeared in her conscious mind. When she was sufficiently calmed and freed from these obsessive, compulsive symptoms and paranoid trends that were causing her inadequate defenses against anxiety and panic, we were able to proceed with therapy.

Without going into the procedure, technique and details of the treatment I gave her, it can be said that Kate's primary need and greatest relief came when she felt and could see that I not only understood what was happening to her but was definitely interested in hearing what she had to say. The initial skepticism she demonstrated diminished and soon gave way to trust and confidence. Gradually she relaxed and was able to tell me, without fear of being laughed at, what she was really thinking.

One of her thoughts was a wish to be President of the United States, because she was sure that if anyone else were President he wouldn't know the most important thing to do to safeguard our country. She would establish garrisons immediately to protect the milk supply. The most important thing to a nation, she told me earnestly, was the milk, because it is milk that children need and children are the future of the nation.

Next, as President, she would organize systems of safeguarding the buses. The traffic lights were very confusing, and the bus drivers weren't sufficiently trained to drive buses in which children were being taken to school. She had watched these drivers very carefully, she said, and they were not thinking about what they were doing. They didn't realize that they had the lives of little children in their hands. A bus driver, she went on, was just as important as a father or mother, and if she were President she would have every bus driver carefully examined. She also conceived of a special army made up of children. It would be a very large army, big enough so that if the grownups wanted to make trouble for them the children could defend themselves.

I tried to get her to talk about her parents and her sister. When she told me how good and kind and loving they were, and how she loved them, I made the mistake, which of course I soon corrected, of implying that she wasn't telling me everything. At this point, she developed an anxiety that let me know that if I continued along this course, the unconscious hostilities would break through and we would be back to where we were before I administered the electrotherapy. After that, I scrupulously avoided discussions of the family and let her work out her problems with society in general, with myself as a vehicle.

This is a clear instance of how a child transfers her attitudes from the parents to society. The grievances against the parents that the child cannot begin to accuse them of, much less correct, because of the terrible retributions that he might have to endure, are worked out in the broader, less dangerous area of society and its institutions. Perhaps, in Kate's case, this was the basic reason that the area of the family had been so unapproachable. Whatever the attitude towards society, whether constructive or destructive, it originates in the family relationship.

There were two significant features represented in the inner milieu of Kate. One was her mother and the other her grandmother. Della, Kate's mother, was the unfortunate victim of a cold, desexualized, isolated and, of course, completely disinterested and unknowing mother. She had never been allowed to develop her own motor apparatus that would have built consciousness for her; therefore she was never able to break her attachment to her mother. In her strivings to achieve for herself the good warm mother she did not have, her affliction caused her to make herself subservient, base and degraded to all of her friends. She let them know they could abuse her, use her and frighten her—in short, achieve their relative comfort at her expense. After she had established a relationship with them in which she was so masochistic, she had to avoid them. In brief, Della created a world of indifferent, cold, cruel mothers whom she would then try, in her feeble way, to change and make into the good mother she was longing for.

She did the same thing with Kate. She reproduced her original sick, cold, aggressive mother in her child—the child, Kate, who had to stay as much as six feet away from people, and who had to say to her mother and to others that she hated them.

In her inner self, Kate wanted to reform the bad mother. She wanted to make the incompetent competent, as we saw in her serious wish to keep a watchful eye on the milk and to maintain forces that would protect her and all children against hostile influences.

Kate, of course, lived in an economy of emotional impoverishment. Her mother overidentified with her, and her personal needs were unknown. The father was too much impaired and consumed by the insatiable needs of his wife, and too inactivated by Della's controlling tendencies, to give the child the loving direction she required. Besides, what Della had to do with Kate was too deep, too significant, too much of a life-and-death struggle for her to be able to tolerate any interference on the part of her husband. It was only because of the understanding and influence I had with Della, and the insights she gained in analysis, that I could get her to cooperate with me and allow me to give Kate a father figure with whom the child could have a relationship with enough color in it so that the child could have, on her horizon, the goal of some day achieving a substitute for me.

This is not meant in any sense to deprecate Kate's own father, who could not possibly, regardless of how much talent and strength of mind he had, cope successfully with this complicated and distorted arrangement of relationships which circumstance had brought into his life.

On the unconscious level, Della was actually very resentful and jealous of what I did for Kate, but because of my encouragement and treatment Kate was becoming the well one to whom her mother would no longer be able to transmit, and so rid herself of, her own mental sickness.

While Della was in treatment with me, I had not reckoned that in transmitting or giving back the sickness her mother had given to her, she would use not her mother, who was the original sick one, but her own child's symbol systems to rid herself of the material her mother had given her. Now, when the child was being cured, the sickness would be returned to Della again. When this situation came about, it had to be made clear to Della that, on the higher levels and using her higher faculties, seeing her child sick was not necessary in order for her to feel well.

The happy end results in this case could not have been achieved if I had not worked with, and had the help of, Della, who gained insight from her analysis. In my estimation, Kate would otherwise have spent the rest of her life in an institution; but because her mother had been analyzed and was able to help we were successful in bringing about developments that made this child happy, not only within herself, but outwardly to the extent that she became one of the best pupils in her school.

Years later, when I saw Kate for a few sessions during her adolescence, she said to me: "It's difficult to describe how really happy our family is. None of my friends has the understanding we have with each other in our house."

Still another instance of the evil effects of riddance from mother to child is the case of Donald. He was a precocious boy, with an IQ far above the classification of genius. At the age of about fourteen, he was referred to me because he had suddenly begun to fail in school and to withdraw from his classmates and his family. His failure was so shocking to his teachers and parents that their reaction shocked him into being even more of a failure.

I established a rapport with him easily when he became aware of the fact that I was not at all surprised by the bizarre change in him. It is remarkable to observe how a patient can become calm when he senses breadth and depth of understanding in his analyst. To children, it is as though they were suddenly taken away from the threats imagined in darkness.

It was not difficult, either, to find out why Donald was failing. He told me quite frankly and honestly. It had dawned on him that his classmates disliked him. They called him either "fat ass" or, even more derisively, "The Brain." To gain their favor and approval, he set out deliberately to make himself ignorant. He told me that when one of his classmates asked him a question about any of the subjects in school he knowingly gave the wrong answer and feigned stupidity. Thus he made himself smaller in order to get the affection that he got from his mother when he complied with her wish to make him less than she was.

The rejections of his classmates recalled to him the early deprivations, humiliations and abandonments by his mother. She was in business with her three old-maid sisters, who all lived in his home. Donald was alone all day, but in the evening he was overwhelmingly adored, cared for and flooded with the affections, subtle sensualities and fantasies of his mother and the three aunts, who treated him as their Prince Charming. His father was crippled by a congenital clubfoot, and although he was a very loving man he offered no actual masculine dominance for a son to identify with. Donald was the prince of the women in his family, but he was the "little" prince. They called him Tiny Boy and catered to him as one does to a great figure—or a feeble one.

The three aunts strove to outdo one another in benevolences and grandiosities. There was little chance for Donald to initiate or to test any donative capacities within himself. Five people were constantly putting into him. He grew to feel as though there were great spaces within himself that had to be filled, and he filled them during the day when his five givers were not around by devouring all the literature he could lay his hands on. The high IQ, of course, was compensatory.

The Analyst and the Children

It became completely unbearable for Donald not to be showered with affection and attention. He needed the same kind of warming and cradling that he had got as an infant, and when he failed to get it in school he established ignorance as the equivalent of vacuity. He withdrew so that things and people would come towards him. He developed the same negative suction that a girl does at about the age of puberty. When the good things were not forthcoming, he felt that the badnesses which were the result of his own breaking-down processes were the riddances or the noxious materials given to him by those he was accustomed and expected to receive from. His parents and aunts, who gave him so much of what they wanted to give, were really giving him destruction. They were destroying his initiative and his motor apparatus by not giving him a chance to use them. They were, indeed, destroying his consciousness.

When he first began treatment with me, his fantasies were homicidal and suicidal for the most part. He experienced shame and guilt because he identified receptivity and passivity with femininity. His feelings that he wanted the boys to love him frightened him, because he felt the boys were looking at him as though he were a "fairy," a title the implications of which he knew from his wide reading and from vulgarizations of the subject, a thoroughly discussed topic of conversation among the boys. His repudiation of his knowledge was not only to win the favor of his classmates but to dispose of his mentality, which might otherwise prevent him from getting the babying he had become addicted to. Most important of all, however, it was a token equivalent of his self-destruction.

In his regression, he was either getting killed by not receiving nurturing or not getting killed by receiving it. In previous chapters, we saw how the infant disposes of his disintegrated substances by disintegrating the mother while he gets her love and feedings. Similarly, when Donald felt hungry for affection and love he assuaged himself by fantasying the dismemberment of one of his parents, or his aunts, or himself.

When he relaxed by identifying with my depth and breadth of understanding and stopped being frightened by his own unconscious fantasy, and when I allowed him to continue expressing these morbid fantasies and impulses, he began to build his own motor apparatus. The simple difference between fact and fancy became clear to him, and as time went on he became less and less frightened by these primitive, unconscious adaptive devices.

Donald had developed into a female because his aunts and parents had made him so on the psychic, symbolic level; consequently he offered to any and all associates that they take the role of the male. I recognized his utterances and did not impugn, degrade or condemn them but listened to them as though they had a future, which they did. When I did this, Donald began to eliminate them, much as a child eliminates riddances and then, as time goes on, begins to control them, to separate them from other parts of himself, and place them where they belong, so that he can go on and develop other, more advanced abilities and talents.

The subtle implications that he didn't have, and therefore had to be given; that he wasn't able to do for himself and therefore had to be done for; that he wasn't able to give and therefore had to be given to; and that he wasn't able to provide and so was abundantly provided for by his working father, mother and three aunts—all this had paralyzed him.

All that was needed to restore Donald was the same thing that is necessary in the atrophy of disuse. The member that is atrophied is simply used. Donald was encouraged to use his mind. He came to know that to forfeit it or surrender it, even voluntarily, was to lose the most valuable asset an individual has—his mind, which gives him freedom to will and independence of action to be creative. It is God's greatest gift.

In discussing children, we hear all about us the euphemism, "They'll grow out of it." Thus many sad and unfortunate developments taking place in our children before our eyes are set aside with a wave of the hand. The "growing out of it" is what the parent has done by having transmitted it to the children. The child is housing the disturbance, and the parent makes believe he knows nothing about it and appears as innocent as Jimmie appeared after he repressed the knowledge of having set fire to his brother's crib.

The Analyst and the Children

From the social point of view, and in accordance with the principle we live by, to accuse these parents of malevolence or any ill-doing toward their children would be useless and unjustified, for "they know not what they do." In most instances, the fathers and mothers of disturbed children cannot be dealt with. They deny, resist and turn their backs on any suggestion that they should look to themselves for the cause of their child's disturbance. When such a thing is suggested, they leave the office of the doctor with outraged dignity and take their child with them.

There are situations in which the child acts out the aggressions on society. At such times the teacher or the principal will call for the parents and advise them that something should be done. At such meetings, the parents are keenly alert for any insinuation that might be made about their dereliction and very soon are so loud in their indignation and protestations that it is not economical for the public servant—teacher or principal—to press the issue, particularly when these scenes are accompanied by violent threats of retaliation for the supposed "insults" given them.

I myself have been the target of terrible rage and hatred from my own patients when I have attempted to provide them with insight into the fact that their children are being made the vessels for their psychic riddances. When such insights are given before higher faculties are developed, the rage and hatred, the instinctual response to being frightened, are inevitable. If they cannot find a symbol system to dispose of what endangers their living integrity in their conceptions of themselves, it is tantamount to their being condemned to death. Then how can we expect the unknowing ones in their striving towards survival to do anything more than defend themselves? The harm has been done to them by their antecedents, and they claim the right, because they have to do it, to do it in turn to their descendants.

Even if the parents are submissive and agree that something must be done, the help they can get from well-meaning but untrained people to clarify what is transpiring in their child's mind is a drop in the bucket. The only hope is that man must continue to strive toward realistic knowledge, and fortunately nature has provided him with the physical endowment to accomplish it.

Chapter 2

Man Whole and Fractional

If a man could be a whole man, which would enable him to be a good lover, a good husband and father, there might be less need for psychiatrists and psychoanalysts. But men have been weakened, and women are starving for the want of their strength.

The religious doctrine that God made Eve out of Adam's rib has wise symbolic implications. The implied idea is that man has to femininize his woman, otherwise she herself must aspire and function not only as a woman but as a man, to complete herself. If there are no men around, or if a man isn't much of a man, she may also find it necessary to specialize her fractional masculinity within herself in an attempt to make it total.

But when she strains her unendowed organism to achieve the amount of masculinity that life situations and some husbands demand of her, the recourse she takes and the resources within herself that she discovers and taps for power tend to be destructive rather than creative. Biologically, on the physical level, she is constituted to be man's counterpart. When she tries to be psychically what she is not biologically, she is endeavoring to achieve the impossible. And what is the opposite of constructiveness and creativity but destructiveness?

A whole man is unfrightened, confident in his ability to function normally and naturally, able to perform the sexual act sympathetically and altruistically by doing the giving, physically and mentally, taking from his woman who has so much to give him, and acknowledging her feminine creativeness. He can also use the world around him for whatever it can yield because of what he himself is able to contribute. The whole man is not beset by doubts. He is motile, agile, upright, goal-directed, confident and peaceful. He needs to make no protest that he is the giver or to feel any shame that he is the taker. He finds himself an ordered body placed in a suitable niche in nature's eternal orderliness.

The whole man is as bilateral and symmetrical in his mind as he is in his physical being, and his functioning is equally harmonious. He is the one who does the loving. This capacity comes as naturally to him as receiving love does to a woman, when each reaches the period of mature sexuality. Anatomically, as the female senses in her reproductive organs a capaciousness in which there is a feeling of call, so the male has urges to yield to the call as he is drawn to fill the capaciousness. If this natural state expands itself through his being and becomes his way of life on the psychic level, his natural tendency is to express—and continue forever to express and deliver—life, warmth, and happiness, all of which come under the heading of love.

This is no romantic or philosophical speculation. This is biology and therefore true, postulated as a principle upon which normalcy can be predicated. The children of such a couple inherit nature's beauty and harmony and so are able to transmit them.

But unfortunately this has not always been our inheritance. Though we theoretically ourselves can become ancestors, able to undo, set to rights and repair all the unilateral situations, asymmetries and distortions that have been our heritage, in the mind of the realistic analyst this is impossible to achieve in the space of a life. It can, however, be the theme of our aspirations. We can dream, fantasy, think about it, and then work towards it. Some day it may be the way our descendants will live, and we can, through identification with them, experience the glow of this realistic hope. This is faith, based on man's own conscious will, his creativeness, judgment, foresight and actual effort. This is faith in a real truth.

To understand better how we may accomplish what is possible for us in our lives, let us return for a moment to a previously stated concept. Life is distinguished from death as an occurrence that comes and goes. As it comes it builds, and when it goes it disintegrates. In nature's innumerable families, there is variance not only in class, size and mode of living but in the time span allotted to each one. There is also variance within the particular species—that is, in the individual's living being. Integration and disintegration follow laws, not all of which are known or understood. The laws we do not know about may cause cohesiveness to be impaired, or not to be maintained, so that integration gives way to disintegration wholly or in part. It can be said, however, that vitality is a characteristic which seems to imply durability. To be sufficiently vital is to be of longer duration in the cohesive and integrated state that is life. It spells out in our imaginations the ideals we have talked about.

Man's highest faculty, his mind and his ego, can be cohesive and integrated, as is his body, or it can become incohesive and disintegrated. When this latter state occurs, there are displacement, disassociation, scattering, fragmentation, all of which are the features that characterize disorganization or mental disorder. Since man's body and its function depend completely, in every detail, on the highest faculties in his mind, he cannot be a whole man if his mind, which is the reflection of his body, does not reflect back to it the true image of himself.

We have seen that a man's mind can be projected from two directions: from within himself (his inner world), and from without, which is the projection of how others see him. He may come to see himself as a caricature of himself, as in the distorted mirrors of a fun house. But if it is his misfortune that the mirrors which are the eyes of his family have a need to disarrange, disfigure and distort him, and disallow him his creativeness, reproductivity and sexual potency, although he may be perfect in his physical structure he cannot then enjoy the mental representation of it in the form and shape of his symbols.

This person, as distinguished from the one who was born as a rare anomaly in nature—that is, with the absence of his physical brain— feels himself unconsciously to have been wronged by those he was born to, and, having been so misused, feels he can be righted again. Such a person, when he has the means available to him, goes to an analyst who can undo the misshaping, the disfiguring, the distortions and the desexualization that have been predatorily inflicted upon him, and from which he is suffering because he cannot rid himself of these sickening superimpositions.

It is disastrously true that a great many people are prevented from visiting an analyst because to them it would be an admission of defeat. This is the failure they have been suffering from and denying. But it would be much better for them if they could admit to it, face it, and try to overcome it. If they could stop deceiving themselves, pretending there is nothing wrong, they could begin to know what it is that plagues them. Instead of defeat, there would be an initial victory.

The realization that there is something wrong with their highest faculties is such a threat to these people that it can be compared only with the feeling of disintegration and imminent annihilation the infant experiences if his mother fails to appear when he is hungry. When that happens, as we have seen, nature provides the infant with the ability to hallucinate, and he achieves security by drawing on the memories of the stimuli of previous sustenances. Similarly, man deceives himself by denying there is a dearth within his mind and in his symbols of prospective optimism about his survival ability, potency, and viability in his conceptions of himself. He makes believe there is nothing lacking.

Yet if he understood what neurosis is he would not be deceived. A neurosis is a condition in which the adaptive system of the individual does not perform adequately for sufficient and healthy gratification in his essential transactions with the outside world of reality.

If others imply, dictate or suggest to an individual that he is off-balance, he begins to limp in his fantasy and logic. Then the world around him, and its natural phenomena that are projected into him and determine his theories, are projected back in illogical and irrational terms that the analyst perceives and uses as tracers that guide him to the origin of the patient's distortions.

There is much justification for the patient's deceiving himself about his rightness. The odds have always been tremendously and overwhelmingly against him. As an infant and child, he had no rights, no recourse. He was absolutely helpless in the hands of those who could, and would, do with him as they wished. In this subsocial period, any attempt to argue his cause with grownups had absolutely no chance to be heard, much less justified. The social order is against the subsocial individual, and any thought of his seriously or militantly standing up to it would be as shattering as a tank confronting a man who could only fight with his fists.

A person is neurotic because the childhood he tries to disown and deny will not be disowned and denied. It forces itself upon him, and in his troubled state, whether he is twenty or fifty years old, he still feels that to face the grownup (the analyst) would be as overwhelming as it was during his childhood. He derides the analyst, jokes about him, thumbs his nose at him. But we can be certain that the more he does so the more he fears him, and therefore the more he needs him. Identified as he is with the family, a neurotic sees the analyst as the incarnate reproduction of the original parents who righteously made themselves good at his expense.

To me it is not a strange paradox to say that the strong ones are the weak ones and the weak ones are the strong ones. A man may pride himself on his stability and calm, but he may be living an oxcart life. If he undertook a more complex and extended kind of existence, he too would begin to feel the pressures, and then he might have to stop jeering at the individual who becomes unstable because of the immense demands made upon him and the responsibilities he assumes.

Pride is a powerful influence, and it adapts itself to any kind of situation. A man may be proud of his name and thus not have to be ashamed of his ignorance. He may be proud of his education in order not to be ashamed of his monetary poverty. He may pride himself on his consistency and thus not have to face the shame of being rigid and stubborn. I once had a patient who stood high on his toes as he left the session and asked triumphantly, "Have you ever seen a more neurotic person than I am?"

If the strong man who is exhausted by his undertakings could see through the pride of the oxcart man and know that pride is a defense against shame, as arrogance is a defense against weakness, then he would realize he is not the one to have anything to be ashamed of. It is simply that the oxcart man has found a device to cover up his own unimportance. With this knowledge, the strong man would not be vulnerable to shaming by the smug, satisfied oxcart man. He would have the courage of his convictions and come for help.

When the undertakings of a man necessitate great expenditures of psychic energy, or the development of thinking at a higher level of complexity, he usually ends up by being the rich breast by which a family and relatives are nurtured.

An analogy may be made here between a sensitive instrument and a blunt one. Sensitivity is the attribute that makes for a truly alive, vibrant, creative personality; the more sensitive the man, the more susceptible he is to feeling, and, conversely, the more insensitive he is, the less susceptible he will be to disturbances, for where there is no sense there is no feeling.

Those who are ashamed and afraid to go to the analyst are those who have been intimidated by others who have nothing to develop, but on the contary have much to lose, if the sensitive ones achieve, in addition to their special endowments and genuine accomplishments, the organization and stability that might then enable them to enjoy the fruit of their strivings. The shrewd, cunning, infantile people who live parasitically off the sensitive, creatively endowed ones are simply defrauding the strong of the simple pleasure of enjoying what rightfully belongs to them, so that the strong will continue unquestioningly to supply them with the good things of life that they are soaking up. They fear, and justly, that if the benefactor gains his full health and understanding he will see through their parasitism and they will be forced to do their part and give up their ill-gotten, unjustified soft berth.

Women who are not being creative and not making their contributions either in the arts or sciences or in their homes and to their families utilize these unused energies in ways that spell disaster for the men and children in their families. Their energies are diverted to various kinds of endeavor which their husbands are completely blind to on the unconscious level, even though they are transacted in the open and are known to all women. The list of energy diversions would include envies of one brand or another, self-esteem elements (keeping up with the Joneses), and all those invectives, implications, connotations and transferences from wife to husband by way of the symbol systems, beyond man's awareness, that break him down. This is the level on which the modern Delilah conquers her Samson. A threatening glance from an infantile wife can subdue, or even disintegrate, an industrial giant.

In a sense, man's romantic nature has built a Frankenstein monster for himself. He has to be the great doer and giver, but in so doing he has to deny his woman the privilege and the dignity of giving something back, as the ovum gives to the sperm. This indignity has been going on for much too long. When man became so grandiose and overprotecting, he weakened his woman into a kind of strength that she now uses to retaliate and to weaken him. She has found recourse in an approach to him through his weakness, the result of his sexual potency's having been impugned on the psychic symbolic level. She says to him in effect, "You say to me there is nothing that I have to do, nothing I can contribute, nothing I can create, and you provide me with all the gadgets and expect nothing from me as though I had nothing to give. Well, then I will do the same to you!" Then she proceeds to do so, with her newly developed talent, that of devitalizing him, which she is now doing at a rate faster than man has ever been devitalized in history.

It is up to man—who should be whole, the giver, the doer and creator—not to undignify, reduce and enrage his woman, but rather give her dignity, as the sperm gives dignity to the ovum, which in turn gives dignity to the sperm. In order to do this, man has to achieve wholeness, which means utilizing all his faculties.

Unfortunately, man has either repudiated his higher faculties, forfeited them, or surrendered them to intimidators who got hold of him during his defenseless childhood, so he functions on lower levels and becomes the mentally sick person with no hope (the hebephrenic) or the fighting one (the paranoid) who at least has a chance. The paranoic personality cannot break through by himself the barrier that separates consciousness from unconsciousness. When life is unsatisfactory and he is unhappy; when his moods are forlorn or sick and his relationships poor; when he cannot tolerate others and causes others not to be able to tolerate him; when he has to run away from them and keep changing wives, friends, interests or acquaintances; or when he has to move from place to place, becoming a restless world traveler—he is externalizing his original sick world from which he then has to escape.

This is when he needs the analyst.

Chapter 3

Symbolization, Intuition and Validation

The goal of analysis is to expand consciousness and lead the patient out of the trap of unconscious life (unreality) into the freedom and reality of consciousness so that he may enjoy realistic give-and-take relationships with his family. The analyst sees the whole being of the patient in all of his time perspectives—as an infant and a child and in his present, always bearing in mind the members in his family and his relationships with them. This total approach enables the analyst to keep in view the realistic involvements of the patient's actual living transactions.

In the analysis, the established inner world of the patient—the family of his childhood—gradually emerges. The analyst is identified now with one, then with another, of the figures of the patient's original constellation, and the patient starts reliving, over and over, the original experiences with them. When the analyst is identified with the good-giving mother, the patient's attitudes are loving and his expectations are optimistic. If he identifies the analyst with the feared and hated one, his attitudes, dispositions and expressions are defensive, aggressive, hostile or depressed. These attitudes do not differ in principle from the way he relates in his present life to other people in the world around him.

There is, however, an important difference in that the analyst knows the meaning of his patient's transferred attitudes and reactions. The analyst's goal is to make what was previously unconscious, conscious, so that the unchanging past that has become buried and continues to exist in its original form of hieroglyphics and vague symbols may be translated into the more definitive language of consciousness—that is, realistic words—and then examined with the critical faculties of conscious thinking and judgment.

The patient has been relating to the present with the emotionality of the past. He has retained these emotions to establish and maintain the security he knew as a child. Such an adult may be recognized through the behavior patterns of spite, defiance, rebellion and submission which he presents to all the authority figures he meets or creates, thus re-establishing for himself the original parents who were his protectors. In doing so, he perpetuates childhood. The spite, defiance and rebellion are cover-ups for the shame of dependency. He achieves survival by looking to protectors and caretakers. His goal in the analysis is to make the analyst both of these things.

The patient may be a successful man in industry, in his profession, in the arts. He may be full-grown, even magnificent in his physical being, yet in his emotionality he is the child described. A large part of his personality structure and his energies are given to denying the childish feelings he would be ashamed to reveal—the frailty he felt as a child, the devastating feeling of annihilation when he was scorned.

I have to plan for a building process which may take two or three years before the patient can bear to expose to me and to himself one of the germinal centers of his present untold misery and suffering. When the conscious ego that has been nutured and vitalized in the analysis reaches the repressed complex, it may prove to have been only a trifle that was overwhelming in those early days. It is like the ogre we imagine in the dark room that when we put on the light turns out to be merely the window shade rattling against the pane.

Some individuals, as we have seen, are incapable of getting over their infantilism by themselves. The extreme egocentric, the psychotic, is indifferent to his environment and does not suffer. He is interested neither in his family nor in other people, but only in himself. He is lost to others and makes no bones about it, and he is not interested in analysis.

On the other hand, the neurotic suffers because he is interested in his environment and tries to reach out to it but is so preoccupied with himself that he is pulled in two directions, towards the future and towards the past, becoming exhausted from the dissipation of energy involved in his conflicting tendencies to relate to the present and still finish off his unfinished childhood.

The neurotic cannot enjoy his family, and they cannot enjoy him. His transactions are not well enough defined. He wants to give, but he gives erratically. He wants to take, but he doesn't know how. He argues about irrelevancies and his humors are unpredictable. He cannot be figured out or depended upon or anticipated, so the organization and coordination of the family are constantly disrupted. Strain and tension are always in the air, and the emotional economy of his family is impoverished. There is no peace in his home.

The love such a person is capable of is not mature or creative love. When he says, "I love you," he really means, "I love me, and I want you to love me, too." The neurotic is incapable of giving full interest and devotion, which he wants and tries to give and suffers because he can't give. He knows intuitively that if you don't give, you don't get in return, and the knowledge leaves him forlorn and pessimistic.

The job of the analyst is to help such an individual to finish his childhood. This he accomplishes by guiding the patient to his own natural resources, which the patient learns to tap in order to gain the strength to march into his adult role and live maturely. He comes to see that maturity is much richer and more secure than childhood could ever be.

When he reaches this degree of development through having come to know the vitality and creative abilities that exist within himself, he is able to discern and credit the other members of his family with similar virtues. He then finds for himself, in his present life, the productive and creative affiliates that he had so vainly sought in the form of parent figures.

The growing optimism that is generated by his vitality and creative abilities displaces the pessimism that had flooded his existence. Having found dignity within himself, he is now able to dignify others. He is able to love and be loved and enrich and be enriched by his family.

There are certain truths people should know. One is that unhappiness is a sickness. It is not fate, not a curse, and it doesn't have to be anybody's lot. It is, in fact, an injustice to an individual and to everyone around him if he continues to be unhappy without trying to find out what causes his unhappiness. The youngest infant comes to sense the progression of time and realizes that for every effect there is a cause. This ability to theorize becomes his ability to think, and when the sickness that is unhappiness is upon the individual it is up to him to think what is causing it. Only when he knows the cause can he help himself. Then the next step is to find strength within himself to do something about it, as he would with any other kind of disease.

Unhappiness can be a stagnant habit which extends itself from the mind into the body, causing actual physical sickness. What an individual's relationships are doing to him, and what he is doing to them, must be realistically known and understood.

His situation, too, has to be evaluated and re-evaluated constantly. Life is an open system. The transactions in it make a man well and happy, or sick and unhappy. The world around him, and the conditions under which he lives, are registered through his symbol systems. These systems can misinterpret his realities and confuse his thinking and, as we have seen, render him unable to enjoy the world he lives in.

Most important of all is his realistic, comprehensive ability to relate to the various time spheres. His highest faculties, if they have the cardinal features essential to aliveness and vitality, will give him the ability to overcome gravity in the temporal universe so that he is able to live in his realistic present time. This does not by any means shut out the other spheres of time. The present has to be able to dip into the past and take out of it the profits from experience and utilize them. It also has to be able to project itself intelligently into the future, to anticipate and prepare competently for what is foreseen.

When, one may ask, does the analysis end?

To analyze a situation or an object means to take it apart, to understand what it is made of. In the analysis, the analyst is the guide in an expedition during which the patient comes to know and understand all that made him what he is. When he has learned to analyze himself and what is happening to him, the analysis is turned over to him and he becomes his own analyst, which he continues to be for the rest of his life. This is precisely what Socrates advised his fellow men to do.

It is easy to conceive of infinity when we contemplate nature, so we are not surprised at nature's infinite patience. The best manifestation of this ideal quality can be found in the fact that nature has preserved the organic structure of man's brain for many thousands of years, waiting for him to come to his senses and put it to full use.

We know that a muscle disintegrates in its power and ability to function when it is not used, but it does not completely degenerate. Atrophy of disuse can always be overcome by use. The part of man's mental apparatus that has not been used because of man's tendency to dehumanize his fellow men has been preserved for him by nature. The structure of his brain is intact. It is as though nature were waiting, like a patient woman or an ovum, for activation.

In my experience, when a human being has not used his higher faculties and acts as though he had been paralyzed by an actual disease but is suffering only from a failure in function, I have found that recovery can be complete. The mind is dormant from disuse but it still can be caused to awaken and live and operate again, actively and effectively. When this takes place, I can only contemplate with the greatest reverence that indestructible, wonderful and eternal female—nature.

Index

✐ ✐ ✐ Index

211

Index

Ego, the, 42, 43, 127, 142, 144, 198, 205
Egomania, 134
Electrotherapy, 189
Empathy, 75
Enuresis, 100
Erotic pleasures of living, 45
  transference, 85
Exhibitionist, 91

Family, the, 8, 9, 10, 16, 21, 36, 57, 58, 59, 60, 65, 68, 93, 95, 104, 197
  neurotic, 44, 62, 67, 68, 73, 180, 206
Fantasies, aggressions towards parents, 109, 193
  autistic, 108
  breast-seeking, 83
  homicidal, 193
  of early childhood, 85
  of male and female, 13
Fantasy, 32, 39, 63, 79, 83, 84, 90, 91, 94, 95, 107, 110, 125, 144, 149, 171, 172, 173, 193
Father and son, in psychoanalytic practice, 64
Female, the, 12, 13, 22
Freud, Sigmund, 7, 8, 76
Frighteners, the, 31

Genitalia, dictates of, 172
Gravity, concept of, 5, 81, 86, 120, 174
  in the temporal universe, 98, 207
  pull of (centripetal, centrifugal), 17, 144

Hallucination, 113
Heterosexual relationships, 81
Hebephrenic, the, 202
Homosexual, 70, 140
Hypochondriac, 115

I-alone theme, 19
Indoctrination, 52
Infant, the, 37, 38, 39, 45, 48, 146, 199
Infantile emotional state, 53, 77, 96, 133, 141, 144, 205
  man, 47
  mother, 90
  organ, 113
  power device, 122, 124
  sexuality, 45, 46, 51, 102
  wife, 69, 202
Intimidators, the, 202

Juvenile delinquent, 105

Latency period, 48, 186
Libido, 28
Love, 23, 47, 50, 164
  as security device, 37

Male, unconscious impulses of, 13
Man, characteristics of, 6, 9, 21, 32, 46
  devitalized, 18, 19, 21, 33
  desexualized, 18, 58, 122, 132, 190
  sexual potency of, 20, 198
Man's mind, 18, 33, 34, 35, 198
Masculinity, qualities of, 12

Index

Index